Crosscurrents / MODERN CRITIQUES

Harry T. Moore, *General Editor*

JOHN UPDIKE
Yea Sayings

Rachael C. Burchard

WITH A PREFACE BY

Harry T. Moore

SOUTHERN ILLINOIS UNIVERSITY PRESS
Carbondale and Edwardsville

FEFFER & SIMONS, INC.
London and Amsterdam

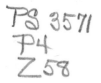
Copyright © 1971, by Southern Illinois University Press
All rights reserved
Printed in the United States of America
Designed by Andor Braun
ISBN 0–8093–0477–5
Library of Congress Catalog Card Number 78–119501

Contents

Preface

John Updike has been called "a major American novelist." Posterity may accept this judgment. Meanwhile we have Updike's books to read, and to us of today they are both timely and lively. He handles language with a careful neatness.

His poems may not prove to be "major," but for the most part they are shrewdly entertaining.

John Hoyer Updike (his middle name is that of his mother's family) was born in 1932 in the Pennsylvania town of Shillington, which he writes of as Olinger in his Olinger Stories (1964) and elsewhere.

John Updike attended Harvard, where he was president of the Lampoon. After he was graduated summa cum laude in 1954, he won a Knox Fellowship and spent a year in Oxford at the Ruskin School of Drawing and Fine Art.

After returning to the United States he became a staff writer on the New Yorker, 1955–57. His first book was The Carpentered Hen (1958), a volume of poems. His first novel, The Poorhouse Fair, came out in 1959. In the following year he received the Rosenthal Award of the National Institute of Arts and Letters. His novel Rabbit, Run was published in 1960; this is a notable story of a former basketball player who finds the post-athletic-team period of his life an anticlimax, a theme touched upon by F. Scott Fitzgerald in The Great Gatsby, with the character of Tom Buchanan. But

Updike made use of the situation for his protagonist rather than for a secondary figure.

Updike's next novel, The Centaur (1963), is the story of a centaur in modern America. It had, as I have noted elsewhere, some forerunners in twentieth-century fiction, in such novels as Cyril Hume's Wife of the Centaur (1923) and Murray Sheehan's Half-Gods (1927). For a fuller discussion of these parallels, see my Preface to Larry E. Taylor's Pastoral and Anti-Pastoral Patterns in John Updike's Fiction, in the Crosscurrents/ Modern Critiques series. There I point out that Updike perhaps had never heard of the centaur books by Hume and Sheehan, but that he was at least following a certain tradition. (There was once even a Centaur Bookshop in Philadelphia.) In any event, John Updike did very well with the centaur theme, and his novel won the National Book Award for Fiction in 1964.

Of the Farm (1965), a short novel, seemed to me to have no ending; it seemed just a beginning, though a charming one. Couples (1968), Updike's fifth novel, is one of those books which have adapted extreme sexual candor in the wake of the legal clearances of Lady Chatterley's Lover and The Tropic of Cancer. Just where Couples will stand in the future is a difficult guess today. Now Updike has published Bech: A Book (1970), a collection of stories, most of them from the New Yorker; it has a unity which makes it seem like a novel; it concerns a Jewish writer whom most reviewers identified with Updike himself.

He is not Jewish, however; he is among the few leading American writers who admit an affiliation with organized religion: he lists himself as a Congregationalist. Politically, he says, he is a Democrat. He lives in Ipswich, Massachusetts, with his wife (the former Mary Pennington) and four children. His neighbors there have apparently not resented his candor in treating the sex life of a small community in Couples.

He formerly did his writing away from his living quarters in a room above a bakery in Ipswich. Now he has moved his "studio" out of town, to a house on the marvelously named Labor in Vain Road. But he will not be laboring in vain if he keeps on producing first-class writing.

HARRY T. MOORE

Southern Illinois University
October 31, 1970

Acknowledgments

Grateful acknowledgment is extended to Random House, Inc. for use of quotations from the works of John Updike, in copyright. Quotations also reprinted by permission of André Deutsch Limited Publishers from the following works of John Updike: *Assorted Prose; Telephone Poles; Rabbit, Run; The Centaur; Of the Farm; Couples; Olinger Stories; Pigeon Feathers; The Same Door; The Music School.* Quotations from *The Poorhouse Fair* reprinted by permission of Victor Gollancz Ltd.

Quotations from *The Carpentered Hen and Other Tame Creatures* by John Updike: "An Ode," "March: A Birthday Poem for Elizabeth," "An Imaginable Conference," "V. B. Nimble, V. B. Quick." Copyright © 1955 by John Updike. Originally appeared in the *New Yorker.* "Scenic," "Capacity." Copyright © 1957 by John Updike. Originally appeared in the *New Yorker.* "Mr. High-mind." Copyright © 1956 by John Updike. Originally appeared in the *New Yorker.* "Mountain Impasse," "Zeppelin." Copyright © 1958 by John Updike. Reprinted by permission of Harper & Row, Publishers, and by permission of Victor Gollancz Ltd.

Appreciation is extended to Houghton Mifflin for permission to quote from "Mass Society and Post-Modern Fiction," by Irving Howe, reprinted from *Recent American Fiction,* ed. Joseph Waldmeier. Quotations also reprinted by permission of Charles Scribner's Sons from *The Eternal Now* (1963) by Paul Tillich.

Quotations from "The Absurd Man As Saint: The Novels of John Updike," by David Galloway. Reprinted from *Modern Fiction Studies,* Vol. 10, Summer 1964. *Modern Fiction*

John Updike: Yea Sayings

1

Perspective

What makes the writer John Updike so popular that before the printer's ink is dry on a new volume of his it is being discussed in high school classroom, college seminar, and pulpit? How can a young man who has hardly lived long enough to know what life is all about compete for attention with the literary greats who spent a lifetime inscrolling manuscripts and a generation or two in their graves before anyone discovered their value or included them in academic or theological discussions? Why is it that from the thousands of manuscripts published each year (to say nothing of the tons of unpublished ones) those of one young writer will be a sure thing in the book market? What is it about John Updike that allows for him almost unprecedented success in an age of unparalleled competition?

It was questions like these which prompted me as early as the publication of *Rabbit, Run* in 1960 to begin reading Updike. I wanted to know the recipe for his—even then—phenomenal success. Having read the brief novel —which I did not particularly enjoy and which did not seem to have the usual qualities of a best seller (which it promptly became)—and several articles by well-known critics whose opinions ranged from extravagant praise to downright insult, I concluded that a new literary great was about to emerge. It was not judgment of his work but the fact of the controversy about it which led me to this conclusion. However, no critical controversy could be given the credit for the popularity which Updike has continued to enjoy since 1960. Even then it was evident that there was something about the man and his work which promised the remarkable. The flowering of genius is a phenomenon I wanted to observe closely. That wish is being granted and has resulted in this volume of criticism.

That the complete unfolding of the Updike genius has been witnessed at this time is, of course, doubtful. Chances are that another Updike volume will appear before this book of criticism is in print and that judgments made here will eventually become obsolete in light of new trends in Updike's writing. Prolificacy and change are as certain for this author as is success. It seems safe, however, to assume that something of what can be discovered at this point in his writing career after the publication of one book of assorted prose pieces, two volumes of poetry, three books for children, four collections of short stories, and five novels will be valid for some time, even after new Updike works are in print.

Updike's insight into human personality, his powers of observation, and his unique style could, without other considerations, give him the status he enjoys, but there is something more which makes certain his success. John Updike has something to say. Much of what he says is still in the form of questions, but they make sense to young searchers. He asks questions about the meaning of life in our time—*now*. He searches for religious definitions to fit the present. He seeks answers to the age-old questions about man's relationship to man, the existence of God, and the relation of the individual to Him. He asks about immortality—all in such a way that even the agnostic listens. He makes it meaningful to ask anew the questions for which the usual answers are quickly invalidated by change in man's perspective. Updike is a resolute and honest searcher.

To those questions for which he finds no answers, he

gives new dimension. The questions take on fresh significance. The search itself becomes worthy of consideration.
Updike wastes no time on frivolous questions but leaves
no pebble unturned and no sound unattended in his
search for answers to important ones. And where there
is an answer—even an unintelligible whisper of an answer—the undertone is worth one's strained attention,
for the question will have been a vital one. The search
is one of integrity. Who can fail to listen, especially
when the rhetoric is that of a gifted artist whose answers
have a propensity for truth?

Classifying Updike by means of conventional social or
religious labels would be misleading if not impossible,
but in a broad sense, there are recognizable influences
evident throughout his work. He is Christian on the one
hand, yet twentieth-century skeptic on the other. He is
a humanist, believing strongly in the worth of the individual, yet finding him often defeated by forces beyond
his control. In the constantly changing American scene,
Updike prizes and holds tightly to some Protestant
American values out of the past while casting off others
as superstitious, outmoded nonsense. Frank Kappler includes him among the existentialists in a statement
about those pessimistic philosophers of despair. He believes that their concept of "alienation" has had "the
most powerful influence on post-war artists and writers
. . . [and that] Updike has increasingly dealt with the
alienated heroes." [1] Kappler's judgment is accurate, and
yet coupled with the despair of Updike's lonely heroes is
a sense of optimism and hope which leavens the author's
work. Life's heavy realities give it body, but a certain
buoyancy lightens it, makes it palatable. His writing is,
in his own words, "necessarily ambiguous." [2] If there
were no contradictions, there would be no questions, no
need to search. If he were labeled Existentialist, Humanist, or Christian, much of what he says would have

to be ignored. The influences of these and other philosophies are evident; none is offered as a final interpretation of life. Updike offers few conclusions. He presents man and society as he sees them, God and Good as he is compelled to believe in them. With his characters and his readers he seeks further understanding, new revelations. John Updike is the voice of today's honest searchers and a literary artist unsurpassed in the current American scene. His is a flowering genius which deserves to be noticed and, judging from the popularity of his books, is being intently observed from its roots to full blossom.

Part of the formula for literary criticism is the task of locating a writer in relation to his contemporaries. How does he rank with other authors of significance? Whose influence is most obvious in his philosophy? Whose ideas does he parrot or expand? The answer is that unless it is at the top, Updike has no "place." He is unique. He imitates no one and competes with nothing but his own output. He shadows no writer and reflects only faintly the glow of several modern theologians. His ideologies are a composite of too many for definition. He is his own best example, moving one step up on the foundations of his own accomplishment each time a new book appears. His earliest writing grew out of his personal experience. He has yet to write about people or events outside the range of his own environment or that of his close contemporaries. As yet he has not touched on racism or war, primary topics in contemporary fiction. His focus is on man searching—not a unique theme but one uniquely handled from volume to volume. John Updike is a unique artist. Perhaps this is the fact which justifies the attention given his work during the past decade.

Because the works of a prolific writer like John Updike tend to cover a broader range than can be judiciously examined in a study of this kind, the major consideration in this volume is given to his poetry and fiction. The children's books and collected essays are not discussed at length. But because nothing an author writes can be entirely overlooked if one would understand his significance in the contemporary scene, a brief survey of one slender volume for children and miscellaneous collected prose is in order.

A sampling of Updike's wit, intelligence, theological leanings, and opinions of other literary figures can be found in *Assorted Prose*. Covering a broad range of topics in pieces written over about a ten-year period which roughly parallels the first decade of Updike's publishing career, *Assorted Prose* can best be described as a collection of nonfiction prose, hopeful in character.

It contains under the title "First Person Plural," a number of his light, witty "Talk of the Town" articles which were first published in the *New Yorker* and which introduced Updike to the American reading public between 1955 and 1957 as well as other pieces which appeared intermittently through 1965. Updike explains in the foreward that the narrators are "a collection of dazzled farm boys" (vii), and the reader recognizes them as different moods of one John Updike. The brief pieces are basically pleasant reports of sights and sounds of New York City but include everything from tongue-in-cheek comments on bees and beer cans to the nightmare of the assassination of President Kennedy in 1963. The section includes tributes to an assortment of famous people: T. S. Eliot, George Bernard Shaw, Gordon Cooper, John Marquand, Grandma Moses, Dwight Eisenhower. With a few exceptions, the selections in "First Person Plural" are a prose lyric to the good things and the good people in New York and the Nation.

The best of Updike humor, in fact, almost all of it, is collected in *Assorted Prose* with the choice pieces under title of "Parodies." Only a very small percentage of Updike's published works to date fall in the category of humor, a fact which may seem surprising since the author has been identified by many as a "humorist." Nothing is further from the truth. A few poems, a limited number of short stories, and the sketches originally published in the *New Yorker* are the sum. The novels which comprise the greater bulk of his work are highly serious. There is comedy here and there as a result of fiasco in the serious events of life; there is, of course, a blending of the humorous with the pathetic, the funny with the sad, all relating the comedy of living. There are hilarious moments and, especially in *Couples*, scenes which border on burlesque, but the undercurrent of meaning is anything but comic. The bulk of Updike's work is earnest portrayal of people whose business is the serious business of life.

If one wonders why a man who, like Updike, *can* write excellent humor but *doesn't*, the author's own words will readily explain. In "Beerbohm and Others," a review of an anthology edited by Dwight Macdonald, he says:

Laughter is but one of many potential human responses; to isolate humor as a separate literary strain is as unnatural as to extract a genre of pathos or of nobility from the mixed stuff of human existence . . . when, as in this century, the absurd, the comic, the low, the dry, and the witty are reinstated in the imaginative masterworks, then humor as such runs the risk of becoming merely trivial, merely recreational, merely distracting. (255)

The sketches included under title of "Parodies" are principally satirical comments on bureaucracy, social refinements, modern art, and contemporary writers. Only high humor is employed: the disciplined phrase, the subtle irony, the controlled hyperbole, the polished perplexity of pun and paradox—all of such quality that, though limited in number, they have earned the title of humorist for their creator even though he perhaps would not claim it for himself.

Neither would he, probably, consider himself a literary critic, but criticism he has written. The reviews in *Assorted Prose* are not without value to the Updike student. They reveal much about their author which his fiction, for example, cannot. Covering about one-third of the volume of *Assorted Prose*, they offer a glimpse of the vast other world of literature with which Updike is familiar. In this section are surely no fewer than a hundred writers to whom the author makes direct reference and obviously knows well, to say nothing of the hundreds more to whom he refers indirectly. Since written reviews probably reveal only a sampling, the reader can speculate on the wealth of literary acquaintance of John Updike.

The section in *Assorted Prose* entitled "First Person Singular" includes six sketches which, roughly chronological, give periodic glimpses of the author's childhood and young manhood. They do not form a complete history, of course, but help to acquaint the reader with the man, Updike, only lightly obscured by fictitious names. Updike's parents are also introduced in these sketches and are quickly recognized as the same people—or closely related to—principals one meets frequently in several of the short stories and two of the novels. The fact that there is no clear line between reality and make-believe when Updike and his parents are concerned adds to the pleasure of speculation in reading the frankly biographical sketches as well as those camouflaged in fiction. For the reader interested in discovering Updike the *man* before Updike the *artist*, "First Person Singular" is the place to begin.

The children's books, *The Magic Flute*, *The Ring*, and *A Child's Calendar* help little in understanding the author. They are not exclusively Updike's creations, for in each case their preparation depended upon or was shared by others. One of these volumes, A *Child's Calendar*, deserves attention because of its antithesis to the usual Updike style and quality. Twelve little poems, one for each month of the year, appear in the accompaniment of quaint illustrations by Nancy Ekholm Burkert. The little book, which can be read in five minutes, of which time much is used in turning pages, is obviously one of those "fringe benefits" enjoyed by the firmly established writer, for, other than the author's name, there is little about the book which justifies publication. The poems— or poem, one long one in twelve sections—are simple little rhymes in iambic pentameter, keyed to the interests and the vocabulary of a small child. "The mud smells happy / On our shoes" (5) suggests a first-grade child's "happiness is" assignment scrawled on yellow newsprint with a crude drawing of what, with the caption, can be recognized as mud. It is a good line—for a child to understand or to write. One stanza in the July calendar is even closer to the kind of verse a child might produce when his teacher asks what he thinks about when someone mentions Independence Day: "America / It makes us think / Of ice-cream cones / And Coke to drink" (13). The teacher's remarks would be kind but less complimentary for the young poet presenting this stanza from the July page: "The shade is hot. / The little ants / Are busy, but / Poor Fido pants" (13).

Updike in "Rhyming Max," a book review included in *Assorted Prose*, says, "Pentameter is the natural speaking line in English . . ." (261), but there seems little that is natural about lines like these which need the artist's skilled touch to relax them. For the work of an accomplished writer, they are embarrassingly rigid. Simplicity can be eloquence. It is obvious that such is what Updike has in mind in A *Child's Calendar*. The images which awake the senses are those a child can understand, for they are taken from his experience and written as he might have written them, simply. But something is missing which would finish them with the delicate perfection ordinarily provided by this poet.

A few lines communicate with the child yet are expressed in a style more in keeping with Updike's usual standards. These are commendable. "And freckles come / Like flies to cream" (11). "The air is full / Of smells to feel—" (17). The adult reader recognizes the familiar Updike theme that God exists at the same time he senses a genuine chill in the stark nakedness of this November stanza: "The beauty of / The bone. Tall God / Must see our souls / This way, and nod" (21).

Except for lines like these, there is very little of the remarkable about *A Child's Calendar*. Fortunately, far more can be said of the two volumes of poetry written for adults.

2

Poetry

Updike's collected poetry, some one hundred twenty selections in two slender volumes, *The Carpentered Hen* and *Telephone Poles*, seems, upon superficial reading, a moderately interesting array of commentaries on a variety of subjects. Few critics mention it except to acknowledge that it exists. Perhaps only after reading all of Updike's works does one discover the significance of his poetry.

Here, as in the novels and the short stories, along with the smiles and the "yea sayings" are the cries of the searcher, the queries of one who seeks rather than answers. Here one finds an adherence to nineteenth-century American Protestant doctrine as well as a present-day probing of the cosmic. Here are humor and serious reflection. Here are gentle satire and sympathetic comment upon the complexities of life. Throughout is the voice of the hopeful seeker—the man who would find, out of the wealth of our religious and cultural inheritance and the startling knowledge of our space age, a religion, a faith, a security for the individual ego.

The first Updike book to appear in print was *The Carpentered Hen* in 1958. The unpretentious little volume announced that a writer of integrity had begun his career. One of the poems, "An Ode" which, according to notes following the title, was "fired into being by *Life*'s 48–star editorial, 'Wanted: An American Novel'" (6) promises that this writer will give an honest account of life, even if his efforts do not meet the requirements pre-

scribed by *Life* for an American novel. In a chant pat-
terned after a Greek triadic ode, the young poet responds
to *Life*'s challenge by pledging a new kind of fiction from
his pen:

An Ode

STROPHE

> *Ours is the most powerful nation in the world. It has
> had a decade of unparalleled prosperity. Yet it is still
> producing a literature which sounds sometimes as if it
> were written by an unemployed homosexual. . . .*

ANTISTROPHE

> I'm going to write a novel, hey,
>> I'll write it as per *Life*:
> I'm going to say "What a splendid day"
>> And "How I love my wife!"
> Let heroines be once again
>> Pink, languid, soft, and tall,
> For from my pen shall flow forth men
>> Heterosexual.

EPODE

> *Atomic fear or not, the incredible accomplishments of
> our day are surely the raw stuff of saga.*

STROPHE

> Raw stuff shall be the stuff of which
>> My saga will be made:
> Brown soil, black pitch, the lovely rich,
>> The noble poor, the raid
> On Harpers Ferry, Bunker Hill,
>> Forefathers fairly met,
> The home, the mill, the hearth, the Bill
>> Of Rights, et cet., et cet.

ANTISTROPHE

> *Nobody wants a Pollyanna literature.*

EPODE

> I shan't play Pollyanna, no,
>> I'll stare facts in the eye:

> Folks come and go, experience woe,
>   And, when they're tired, die.
> Unflinchingly, I plan to write
>   A book to comprehend
> Rape, fury, spite, and, burning bright,
>   A sunset at The End.

STROPHE

> *In every healthy man there is a wisdom deeper than his
> conscious mind, reaching beyond memory to the prime-
> val rivers, a yea-saying to the goodness and joy of life.*

ANTISTROPHE

> A wise and not unhealthy man,
>   I'm telling everyone
> That deeper than the old brainpan
>   Primeval rivers run;
> For *Life* is joy and *Time* is gay
>   And *Fortune* smiles on those
> Good books that say, at some length, "Yea,"
>   And thereby spite the Noes.

Though "An Ode" suggests through gay satire that it would be difficult to write according to the prescription of *Life* editors, by implication it treats the subject of the writer's commitment with gravity. Suggesting that he cannot write a book to comprehend "Rape, fury, spite, and, burning bright, / A sunset at The End," the poet thereby promises integrity. The reader gets the impression, however, that if it is possible to write honestly and at the same time to include a "yea-saying to the goodness and joy of life," this would-be novelist will do it. Updike's first three novels, appearing one by one somewhat later than "An Ode," fulfill the seemingly unreasonable requirements. They draw life as it is and, even in view of its sometimes sordidness, maintain a mood of hope and optimism.

Other poems in this volume comment upon the puzzling complexity of life; suggest that scientific marvels will not, alone, give answer to man's significance; imply that many philosophies have failed us but that religion may still have something to offer.

In "March: A Birthday Poem for Elizabeth" (19–20), the poet anticipates the future for his child who will be born in his own birthday month. He describes March, which is clearly a reflection of the confusing complexity of life as it appears to the poet.

> Clouds stride sentry and hold our vision down.
> By much the same token, agonized roots
> Are hidden by earth. Much, much is opaque.

But, he continues hopefully, it is a good month, a good life, a good time in which to be born. The poem concludes with an exuberant salute to that wonderful complexity, life, which is about to begin once more in a new human being:

> Still, child, it is far from a bad month,
> For all its weight of compromise and hope.
> As modest as a monk, March shall be there
> When on that day without a yesterday
> You, red and blind and blank, gulp the air.

"Scenic" (13), a poem found in the same volume, is, on the surface, a lightly satirical description of life in modern San Francisco. Subjectively, it comments on the complexity of man's existence—its questionable purpose, its comforts, its beauty, and, ironically, at its very core, its defects. The concluding stanza makes the point succinctly:

> Here homes are stacked in such a way
> That every picture window has
> An unmarred prospect of the Bay
> And, in its center, Alcatraz.

Updike includes himself in his commentaries on the nature of man. He finds humankind erring, complex, and various of type and purpose. "Capacity" (24), a sixteen-line poem of one sentence says much about that confusing multiformity called mankind of which the poet is a part.

Capacity

Affable, bibulous,
corpulent, dull,
eager-to-find-a-seat,
formidable,
garrulous, humorous,
icy, jejune,
knockabout, laden-
with-luggage (maroon),
mild-mannered, narrow-necked,
oval-eyed, pert,
querulous, rakish,
seductive, tart, vert-
iginous, willowy,
xanthic (or yellow),
young, zebuesque are my
passengers fellow.

His fellow passengers on the bus, his companions in life, are a heterogeneous crowd of individuals. The reader, dictionary in hand, waits to hear more.

For all their complexities and weaknesses, men mean well, or so it would seem in "An Imaginable Conference" (25), a poem about two *important* people whose conference is interrupted by a most *unimportant* office boy who

apologizes speaking without commas
"Oh sorry sirs I thought" which signifies

what wellmeant wimbly wambly stuff it is
we seem to be made of.

Many of Updike's characters are, indeed, made of "well-meant wimbly wambly stuff," but they are authentic portraits of recognizable human beings, all confused at times, no two alike.

Concepts of right and wrong and the application of justice create another complexity within the puzzle of man's life as evidenced in "Mr. High-mind" (42). The persons who make up the drama of the poem, like those in *The Pilgrim's Progress*, are allegorically named. Mr. High-mind is contemptuous of the other eleven members of the jury which include Lust, Hate, and Superstition. His thoughts soar far above theirs.

> His brain takes wing and flutters up the course
> First plotted by the Greeks, up toward the sphere
> Where issues and alternatives are placed
> In that remorseless light that knows no source.

And after much contemplation,

> High-mind as Judge descends to Earth, annoyed,
> Despairing Justice. Man, a massy tribe,
> Cannot possess one wide and neutral eye,

and he discovers what the poet is trying to tell us, that even High-mind has not solved the impasse but is just one of the "massy tribe." All men are confused and lack the final answers.

> He casts his well-weighted verdict with a sigh
> And for a passing moment is distressed
> To see it coinciding with the rest.

Concepts of good and evil and man's relationship to them create a complexity not solved by the great minds of the past nor the "high minds" of the present.

Another "high mind," that of the "pure" scientist, becomes a subject of light satire in "V. B. Nimble, V. B. Quick" (17), and while we smile with the poet, we also hear his message, which is that science is not enough to answer the enigma of life.

V. B. Nimble, V. B. Quick

Science, Pure and Applied, by V. B. Wigglesworth,
F. R. S., Quick Professor of Biology in the University of
Cambridge.—*a talk listed in the B.B.C. Radio Times*

V. B. Wigglesworth wakes at noon,
Washes, shaves, and very soon
Is at the lab; he reads his mail,
Tweaks a tadpole by the tail,
Undoes his coat, removes his hat,
Dips a spider in a vat
Of alkaline, phones the press,
Tells them he is F. R. S.,
Subdivides six protocells,
Kills a rat by ringing bells,
Writes a treatise, edits two
Symposia on "Will Man Do?,"
Gives a lecture, audits three,
Has the Sperm Club in for tea,
Pensions off an aging spore,
Cracks a test tube, takes some pure
Science and applies it, finds
His hat, adjusts it, pulls the blinds,
Instructs the jellyfish to spawn,
And, by one o'clock, is gone.

Through gay hyperbole the poet tells us that the scientist
has taken some pure science and applied it, but nothing
more. He has told us nothing, solved nothing. He flits
importantly from one routine activity to another, answering no questions for us.

That we might find some clues in nature is suggested
in "Mountain Impasse" (61), which was inspired by
some lines from *Life* with which Updike introduces the
poem: " 'I despise mountains,' Stravinsky declared contemptuously, 'They don't tell me anything.'—*Life.*" In
the poem the mountain and the composer have a conversation, Stravinsky declaring that he finds the mountain

dull and uninspiring. In the final stanza the poet tells us
why the great mind is not able to learn from nature:

> The hill is still before Stravinsky.
> The skies in silence glisten.
> At last, a rumble, then the mountain:
> "Igor, you never listen."

For the student of Updike there is certainly significance in the fact that the final poem in the author's first
volume, *The Carpentered Hen*, looks to religion for
security. "Zeppelin" (82) is the concluding selection in
a group entitled "A Cheerful Alphabet of Pleasant Ob-
jects." In eight short lines the poet reminds us that the
scientific wonders of nations have not solved man's problems and that philosophy, too, has failed us. He does not
declare with dogmatic certainty that religion can help
us, but he does suggest that it may have some answers.
In fact, there is something very permanent about the
stars, even though they are distant and "narrow." Updike equates them with religion's offerings.

Zeppelin

> A German specialty, since men
>   Of other nations must inveigle
> Helium or hydrogen;
>   But Germany had Hegel.
>
> It fell, as do Philosophy's
>   Symmetric, portly darlings,
> Fell from skies where one still sees
>   Religion's narrow starlings.

Updike's second volume of poetry, *Telephone Poles*,
published in 1963, continues the search for meaning in
life. Though only five years of time separate the two
books, three novels and two collections of short stories
made their appearance and impact upon the reading
public in the interim. *Telephone Poles* begins in tune

with the whirling, tumbling, confusing tempo of 1963. Its opening selection, "Bendix" (103), would at first seem to be only a rhyming comment about a familiar household appliance, but the final word of the last line stops the reader short: "apocalypse." Apocalypse, a revelation? a prophecy? The automatic washing machine, unquestionably symbolic of our mechanized age, becomes prophetic of our future as well.

Bendix

This porthole overlooks a sea
Forever falling from the sky,
The water inextricably
Involved with buttons, suds, and dye.

Like bits of shrapnel, shards of foam
Fly heavenward; a bedsheet heaves,
A stocking wrestles with a comb,
And cotton angels wave their sleeves.

The boiling purgatorial tide
Revolves our dreary shorts and slips,
While Mother coolly bakes beside
Her little jugged apocalypse.

Clearly visible to the unobservant woman who "coolly bakes beside," the machine relentlessly turns, tosses, and twists and mixes in one chaotic mass the "cotton angels" (of man's making?) with the insignificant minutiae, the buttons, stockings, combs, of man's existence—in a "boiling purgatorial tide." Does it suggest hopeless confusion of ideas and values in the age of mechanical servants? It seems so. But perhaps the "purgatorial tide" is a necessary preliminary to a more peaceful existence. Is there a note of hope? An apocalypse might be more than a revelation. Webster's first definition reveals more possibilities for Updike's meaning: "one of the Jewish and Christian writings of 200 B.C. to A.D. 150 marked by pseudonymity, symbolic imagery, and the expectation of an imminent cosmic cataclysm in which God destroys the ruling powers of evil and raises the righteous to life in a messianic kingdom." Does the poet subtly suggest that, chaotic as human existence has become, better things are possible? The very fact that he uses the term associated with obscure but hopeful religious traditions suggests that he is optimistic—not for the present, perhaps, but for the future of man.

The insight given us by the "jugged apocalypse" of a chaotic confusion in this life is repeated in several selections in *Telephone Poles*. The poet seems to be saying, "We live in turmoil and indecision. Man is good and man is bad. Man is confused. The world is confused. Man is alone and yet a significant being not altogether hopeless. The universe dwarfs man and yet includes him. Religion as man has practiced it will ever fail him. Change is certain; let one find security in anything and it will as certainly fail him—and yet, and yet, there is hope. God exists." Again as in his first collection of poetry, Updike suggests that the answers may still be found in religion—somewhere. Finally, no conclusion drawn, he assures us that the search itself is rewarding, that contemplation of the mystery of God and man's relation to Him is fascinating.

The poem immediately following "Bendix" is entitled "Reel" (104); it comments clearly on the confusion, the whirling imperspicuity of all things.

Reel

whorl (hwûrl; hwôrl), n. . . . 2. Something that whirls or seems to whirl as a whorl, or wharve . . .
—*Webster's Collegiate Dictionary*

> Whirl, whorl or wharve! The world
> Whirls within solar rings
> Which once were hotly hurled
> Away by whirling things!

Wind whirls; hair curls; the worm
Can turn, and wheels can wheel,
And even stars affirm:
Whatever whirls is real.

We whirl, or seem to whirl,
Or seem to seem to; whorls
Within more whorls unfurl
In matters, habits, morals.

And when we go and carve
An onion or a tree,
We find, within, a wharve
And, in the wharve, a whee!

There are no straight answers about "matters, habits, morals," only reeling ambiguity. Perhaps the answers are found only in the confusion—for "even stars [which suggest permanence in many Updike poems] affirm: / Whatever whirls is real."

The complex universe in which man must find his place is discussed in "The High Hearts" (125). The poet comments wryly on the relative placement of hearts of elephants, giraffes, and men. The two larger animals carry their hearts at a higher level, physically, than does man, but something about man keeps him straining upward, physically and intuitively.

Poor man, an ape, anxious to use his paws,
Became erect and held the pose because
His brain, developing beyond his ken,
Kept whispering, "The universe wants men."
So still he strains to keep his heart aloft,
Too high and low at once, too hard and soft.

The poet is not talking about animal anatomy at all but about man and his search for his rightful place in the universe. For, "The universe wants men," and man "Became erect and held the pose. . . ." that he might understand more of what he perceived. It is not easy for

him. He has not yet attained his footing, his place in relation to all other things in creation, for he is "Too high
and low at once, too hard and soft," but intuitively he
knows he must keep trying and ". . . still strains to
keep his heart aloft."

In his search for a place, man is often very much alone,
as is illustrated in "Mobile of Birds" (159). Again the
universe is the setting; the poet observes the "polycentric
orbits" because "There is something / in their planetary
weave that is comforting." Man, symbolized by a tiny
bird, becomes almost weightless, and yet so significant
that he can balance the weight of many others:

> A small bird
> at an arc's extremity
> adequately weights
> his larger mates'
> compounded mass: absurd
> but actual—there he floats!

Is it the very fact that he is alone—forced to exist at a
distance from his fellows, never reaching them, never
knowing them, that makes him significant? It seems so,
for any change in his position would destroy the balance
of the mobile, the "planetary weave," the plan for all
beings.

In the next stanza we recognize man's shape in "Sil-
houettes" and shadows and learn that his immortal
destiny may be to return and then again to return to the
elements from which he emerged:

> Silhouettes,
> projections of identities,
> merge and part and reunite
> in shapely syntheses—

He is indispensable, essential to the very balance of the
universe, to the complex pattern of all things, and yet
he is alone,

for the birds on their perches of fine wire avoid collusion
and are twirled
alone in their suspenseful world.

Updike makes it clear that man's little but certain significance is strengthened by his own contributions to his
planet. In "Telephone Poles" (139), the title poem of
this volume, he affirms his confidence in man who, now
and then, constructs something useful, something in
ways superior to nature's creations. He says of the telephone poles, "They have been with us a long time. /
They will outlast the elms." They are not entirely beautiful, "These weathered encrustations of electrical debris
—/ Each a Gorgon's head. . . . / Yet they are ours. We
made them." They are well made and more useful than
Nature's trees from which they came.

The Nature of our construction is in every way
A better fit than the Nature it displaces.
What other tree can you climb where the bird's twitter,
Unscrambled, is English?

We lose something in reconstructing nature, for "their
thin shade is negligible," but we at least erase the tragedy
of living and dying with which nature is forever con-
fronting us. There is something valuable in a telephone
pole which does not remind us of the riddle of eternity:

But then again there is not that tragic autumnal
Casting-off of leaves to outface annually.
These giants are more constant than evergreens
By being never green.

If man can improve upon nature, even in so small a way,
he surely is not entirely hopeless.

Improving upon nature may be man's responsibility.
It certainly is not extraneous activity; man is not extraneous. He is a part of all things, we learn again in "Vibration" (166).

> The world vibrates, my sleepless nights
> discovered. The air conditioner hummed;
> I turned it off. The plumbing
> in the next apartment sang;
> I moved away, and found a town
> whose factories shuddered as they worked
> all night. The wires on the poles
> outside my windows quivered in an ecstasy
> stretched thin between horizons.
> I went to where no wires were; and there,
> as I lay still, a dragon tremor
> seized my darkened body, gnawed
> my heart, and murmured, *I am you.*

If he is a searcher, he must voice the question of his place in the universal structure; he must listen to the world's "vibrations" if he is to understand himself. And, vibrating with the universe, he will become a part of its rhythm. He *is* a part of its rhythm. He must recognize this fact and identify with the cosmos if he is to live peacefully in it.

The fear of the unknown expressed in "Vibration" may be related to "cosmic fright" mentioned in "White Dwarf" (110), but again the poet finds security in the permanence of stars, even in their infinity. His fear becomes his comfort, for he can relate his lonely situation to that of the "White Dwarf."

> Discovery of the smallest known star in the universe was announced today . . . The star is about one half the diameter of the moon. — *The Times.*

> > Welcome, welcome, little star!
> > I'm delighted that you are
> > Up in Heaven's vast extent,
> > No bigger than a continent.
> >
> > Relatively minuscule,
> > Spinning like a penny spool,
> > Glinting like a polished spoon,
> > A kind of kindled demi-moon,

You offer cheer to tiny Man
'Mid galaxies Gargantuan —
A little pill in endless night,
An antidote to cosmic fright.

Perhaps it is with tongue in cheek that the poet writes the last lines of "Sonic Boom" (113), another poem suggesting "cosmic fright," but it is certain that he is aware as always of the question of his significance in the cosmos.

Sonic Boom

I'm sitting in the living room,
When, up above, the Thump of Doom
Resounds. Relax. It's sonic boom.

The ceiling shudders at the clap,
The mirrors tilt, the rafters snap,
And Baby wakens from his nap.

"Hush, babe. Some pilot we equip,
Giving the speed of sound the slip,
Has cracked the air like a penny whip."

Our world is far from frightening; I
No longer strain to read the sky
Where moving fingers (jet planes) fly.
Our world seems much too tame to die.

And if it does, with one more pop
I shan't look up to see it drop.

Perhaps even our world is impermanent; most things are, and this fact is part of the reason for the confusion which the searcher encounters at every turn.

Nothing is permanent. Change is the only certainty. For the searcher, even those things which once seemed firm and settled alter through the perspective of time; the complexity of living continues. "Shillington" (154), a poem written about Updike's birthplace, discusses the impermanence of "certain" things:

Returning, we find our snapshots inexact.
Perhaps a condition of being alive
Is that the clothes which, setting out, we packed
With love no longer fit when we arrive.

The "clothes which setting out, we packed / With love . . ." doubtless include the ideas which, when young, we accepted readily, only to find that as we aged and grew more wise, no longer satisfied our needs.

The problem of change in seemingly "Permanent" things of our youth resembles that of religious change over a much longer period as Updike implies in "Comp. Religion" (123). The "Comp." or "comparative" religion suggests more than an academic course. The poet explains that the history of religion "begins with fear of mana" and in the end returns to "mana." In the interim man makes change after change in an effort to fulfill his needs. There are the "Native dances, totems, ani-/ Mism and magicians . . ." the "gods and ziggurats." Eventually religious history brings us to "Puristic-minded sages" who "edit / Their welter into one sweet Will." As in the beginning all power is again embodied in one.

This worshipped One grows so enlightened,
Vast, and high He, in a blur,
Explodes; and men are left as frightened
Of *mana* as they ever were.

The poet-searcher tells us that religion, as men have taught and practiced it, has changed over the centuries but remains an artificiality beginning with fear and ending with fear. Religion fails us because it is man's "welter" or chaotic turmoil interpreted as "one sweet Will." At this depth it has always been inadequate and is of no comfort to the man who seeks Truth.

Man's failure to define God or his own relationship to Him does not mean that there is no God, however. The poet continues his pursuit of Truth. As *Telephone*

Poles is brought to a close, there are three poems which indicate the direction his search is taking. One of them tells us that God exists. Another, immediately following, declares that in Christianity we have either infinite hope or nothing at all. The final long selection of the volume tells us that the great mystery of God and His smallest living creatures is ever being played out before our eyes and that even the mystery, unsolved, is magnificent to contemplate. The search itself is worthwhile.

That God exists is affirmed simply and conclusively in "Fever" (163). The poem is a weightless revelation, the more convincing because it does not deal with philosophic or religious profundities but with certain and unexplained knowledge "hidden from health" and from intellectual and scientific scrutiny.

Fever

I have brought back a good message from the land of 102:
God exists.
I had seriously doubted it before;
but the bedposts spoke of it with utmost confidence,
the threads in my blanket took it for granted,
the tree outside the window dismissed all complaints,
and I have not slept so justly for years.
It is hard, now, to convey
how emblematically appearances sat
upon the membranes of my consciousness;
but it is a truth long known,
that some secrets are hidden from health.

God exists.

The poem following "Fever" is entitled "Seven Stanzas At Easter" (164); it declares that if we are going to accept the Christian concept of God's existence, we must accept it literally, wholeheartedly. In the character of the honest seeker after truth, however, Updike reserves a margin for certainty. He refrains from complete commitment to Christianity even though he seems to be

suggesting that it is the best answer man has yet designed in the riddle of God-to-man relationships. He says,

> Make no mistake: if He rose at all
> it was as His body;
> if the cells' dissolution did not reverse, the molecules
>   reknit, the amino acids rekindle;
> the church will fall.

He does not say, "Christ rose," but "*if* He rose . . .
[italics mine], it was as His body"; he rejects entirely the
apologist's watered-down view of Christianity:

> It was not as the flowers,
> each soft Spring recurrent;
> it was not as His Spirit in the mouths and fuddled
>   eyes of the eleven apostles;
> it was as His flesh: ours.

He urges man to accept the resurrection literally or not
at all. As a symbol of something in which we no longer
believe, it is a mockery. As a reality in which we have a
part, it may be the miracle we have claimed it to be.
Providing an "if" for an emergency exit, he urges us to
"walk through the door. . . . And if we will have an
angel at the tomb, / make it a real angel, . . . lest,
awakened in one unthinkable hour, we are embarrassed
by the miracle, / and crushed by remonstrance." If our
Christian hope is to mean anything, we must take the
story of the resurrection—essentially the basis for Christian doctrine—in its incredibility and in its entirety.

It strikes the reader as highly significant that Updike
has written a poem specifically for Christians and placed
it at a point of importance toward the end of his collection in which he has revealed his search for Truth step
by step. Perhaps it is even more significant that in the
final long selection in the book he tells us that God and
life are still a magnificent mystery fascinating to contemplate. "The Great Scarf of Birds" (173) is a descrip-

tion of an experience which strangely moved the poet. At first he recalls the beauty of a scene about him as he played "golf on Cape Anne in October."

> Ripe apples were caught like red fish in the nets
> of their branches. The maples
> were colored like apples,
> part orange and red, part green.
> The elms, already transparent trees,
> seemed swaying vases full of sky.

But what he saw that day was far more than a colorful and symbolic still life which would have delighted a painter.

As if out of the Bible
or science fiction,
a cloud appeared, a cloud of dots
like iron filings which a magnet
underneath the paper undulates.
It dartingly darkened in spots,
paled, pulsed, compressed, distended, yet
held an identity firm: a flock
of starlings, as much one thing as a rock.
One will moved above the trees
the liquid and hesitant drift.

Come nearer, it became less marvellous,
more legible, and merely huge.
"I never saw so many birds!" my friend exclaimed.
We returned our eyes to the game.
Later, as Lot's wife must have done,
in a pause of walking, not thinking
of calling down a consequence,
I lazily looked around.
The rise of the fairway above us was tinted,
so evenly tinted I might not have noticed
but that at the rim of the delicate shadow
the starlings were thicker and outlined the flock
as an inkstain in drying pronounces its edges.
The gradual rise of green was vastly covered;
I had thought nothing in nature could be so broad but grass.

And then the reader experiences with the poet the moment of significance: a wordless but certain message is delivered direct to his heart by revelation. An incident occurs which can be explained only as "instinctive," and instinctively, intuitively, the poet knows he has seen Omnipresence at work.

> And as
> I watched, one bird,
> prompted by accident or will to lead,
> ceased resting; and, lifting in a casual billow,
> the flock ascended as a lady's scarf,
> transparent, of gray, might be twitched
> by one corner, drawn upward and then,
> decided against, negligently tossed toward a chair:
> the southward cloud withdrew into the air.

What God is, the poet does not know, but the lifting of the "scarf" is clearly His gesture. Even the reader feels that the incident requires no elaboration. It *was*.

What was the message given? Certainty. Certainty of an intelligent controlling force in the universe powerful enough to keep the planets in orbit and particular enough to lift one starling to guide a flock. Upon one fluttered signal thousands rise as they have done since long before man was articulate. The poet does not say that he can verbalize the sudden insight the experience gave him. He can only know that it was given. He knows only that something is there for him to seek. He knows that the mystery of God and His relationship to all creatures is wondrous to contemplate. He concludes:

> Long had it been since my heart
> had been lifted as it was by the lifting of that great scarf.

3

The Poorhouse Fair

Updike's search does not end with his poetry; it only begins there. His first three published novels, *The Poorhouse Fair*, 1959, *Rabbit, Run*, 1960, and *The Centaur*,
1963, each in a unique way describes mankind as confused but capable of goodness, lonely and in need of
guidance but forever seeking it. Each presents some aspect of modern culture on which man has depended but
which has failed him. Yet each, in a kind of youthful
optimism, suggests that if we can only make the right
selections and applications, the best aspects of our cultural, social, and religious heritage can provide for us a
new understanding of ourselves in relation to others and
to God. In each book the possibilities of finding truth
through religion are emphasized over other sources of
guidance. A partly doctrinal, partly mystical search
threads its way through the troubled stories and remains
with the reader as a fragile but shining web of assurance
that there are answers to the problems of man in our
time. The web, like a map uncertainly sketched, urges
the reader on to Updike's next level of search, the less
optimistic novels, and finally to the summit, the short
stories.

The literary critics appraise these earliest novels with
elaborate superlatives and polite restraint, doubts and
condemnation. Their opinions are so numerous and varied that one is forced to make his own evaluations from
careful and complete reading. Stanley J. Rowland, Jr.,
says, "Something is terribly wrong with John Updike—

with his artistic vision and capacity for emotional response." [1] At the opposite end of the scale of opinion, Michael Novak believes that "John Updike has already awakened themes dormant in American letters since Hawthorne and Melville." [2] Such differences of opinion suggest the kind of challenge the reader will find in John Updike's novels.

The search for religious beliefs to fit our time is clearly the tenor of *The Poorhouse Fair*, which made its appearance in 1959. This was just one year after publication of the first volume of poetry, *The Carpentered Hen*, which was discussed in chapter two. *The Poorhouse Fair* is a book of contrasts. It contrasts age and youth, America past and present, Christianity and humanism, religion and science. The studies of contrast all serve as a means of pursuing a more important topic, a search for a religion suitable to and adequate for modern man. As in the poetry, there is an atmosphere of confusion but a prevailing optimism. The author openly and tolerantly examines contradictory philosophies and social institutions. He is sympathetic to all points of view, frequently leaving the reader to make his own decisions if decisions can be made. An objective searcher, he presents both sides of a coin but does not toss it into the air to see which side will land with its face to the sun. He accepts the fact that life is ambiguous; choices cannot easily be made.

Two characters in the story embody most of the contrasts the author presents. Hook, a ninety-year-old resident of a New England poorhouse, represents the past, Protestant Christianity, American individualism, and belief in sin, punishment, immortality, heaven, and God the Father.

Conner, the efficient young director of the government-supported home for the aged, represents the new America (possibly of 1980), practical humanism, collective good, impersonal "goodness," and a certainty that man's life is terminated with its natural, physical death. He believes man can create his own earthly paradise with his own works; there is no soul nor soul's destination and no God. Conner represents the unemotional, the strictly rational thinkers of a self-sufficient modern society.

For both points of view Updike presents a convincing case. It is as if he says, "See, that and that in our heritage we should keep, but *this* in the new culture and *this* are also good. Isn't there some way to keep the best of the old, combine it with the best of the new, and gain a fresh new compound which we have not yet found but which will solve our dilemma?" The thing which is not clear is just which aspects of the new humanism (and science and reason) should replace which factors of the older Christianity. The author seems to cling to his heritage with a deep and tenacious devotion while giving willing ear to a logical and reasonable contradiction. In this ambiguity is found confusion similar to that described in much of his poetry. The conclusions which he draws are tentative, much as they are in the poetry, but they are tinted with the same hope, the same optimism, the same faith in a continuing search.

The arguments between Hook and Conner, the Past and the Present, are handled as systematically as a debate but with much more variety of approach. *The Poorhouse Fair* is, first of all, a story which has a plot, loosely woven but complete; which has several fascinating individuals—not "characters" but real individuals—whose sufferings and joys in life are as real as the next door neighbor's; and which has a setting to please the most demanding for something new. The time is the near future; the place is a home for the elderly in a welfare state. Woven carefully into the fabric of the novel are the arguments, the rebuttals, the redefinitions, and the challenges. The only omission is the decision. The novelist leaves that to the reader, concluding only that the search for a conclusion will go on.

Hook, a very old man, could easily have been nothing more than a symbol, a colorless and uninteresting representation of something ready to die and be forgotten. He is, rather, a living individual, a person the reader meets and delights to see and hear. His speeches are not just verbalized opinions of the author, but are his own thoughts phrased sometimes hesitantly, always economically, and intoned with age and wisdom. We learn from Updike himself one reason that Hook seems real. "I was trying to make an oblique monument to my grandfather; who in the guise of Hook I wished to treat with a tenderness I had never shown the old man himself." [3] Hook is treated not only with tenderness but with unbiased realism and honesty. We can, with Conner,

examine the old man's face as intimately as a masterpiece in a museum: the handsome straight nose; the long narrow nostrils suggesting dignity more than vigor; the dark, disapproving, somewhat womanish gash of the mouth; and the antique skin mottled tan and white and touched with rose at the crests of the cheeks, stretched loosely over bones worn by age to a feminine delicacy. (36–37)

Unlike Conner, we can understand Hook's point of view because of Updike's insight into the old man's character.

One of the subjects for debate between Hook and Conner is the problem of sin and punishment. Hook, in the traditionally Christian interpretation, believes that when man errs, his sin is punished, measure for measure.

"Now in my own life," Hook said, and brought down the edge of his hand upon the chopping-block of the chair arm, "looking back I perceive a mar-velous fitting together of right and wrong, like the joints the old-time carpenters used to make, before everything was manufactured metal and plastic. . . . Ver-y seldom, in my life, did a transgression not bring its own punishment, so that in some cases, as drunkenness, I could not tell where the offense left off and the penalty began. . . . The bookkeeping is far more strict than even that of a Boston banker. . . . Virtue is a solid thing, as firm and workable as wood. Your bitterness"—he looked directly at Conner, his eyes greatly magnified by cataract lenses—"is the wilful work of your heart." (77–78)

Conner, on the other hand, believes that man is neither sinful nor righteous but is either useless or capable of accomplishment of value to himself and to his fellow man. Accomplishment is essentially the counterpart of Hook's "goodness." To Conner, a baby is born neutral, "a bundle of appetites that society, for its convenience, teaches certain restrictions. To enforce these it invokes the supernatural as a mother would an absentee father" (78). As society teaches the neutral infant, that child may become a man capable of great achievement. If society fails, the child becomes not sinful but useless. To Conner there is no sin—only failure to fulfill one's potential. One of man's accomplishments, music, often reminds Conner of man's potential:

He could not hear a dozen chords without crystals building in his head, images: naked limbs, the exact curve of the great muscle of a male thigh, cities, colored spires soaring. Man was good. There was a destination. Health could be bought. (87)

Heaven is, of course, a subject of argument between the two men. Hook comments very little on it, leaving all to faith. He believes. The details of what and where heaven is do not seem to worry him. At one point, trying to comfort a blind friend, he says, "No doubt, Elizabeth, Heaven will be something of what each wants it to be" (73). He does not try to conceive it; he just trusts that it will *be*. He thinks that "the people nowadays have it so good, they are unable to conceive of a better place awaiting them" (117).

Conner, the idealistic humanist, believes the only

heaven man will ever have is one he creates for himself during his lifetime on earth. By contrast to Hook's Heaven, which is planned by God and must be taken on faith, Conner's is the product of the imagination of a social visionary, is as unrealistic as Hook's and more remarkable:

As for my conception of Heaven . . . I see it placed on this earth. There will be no disease. There will be no oppression, political or economic, because the administration of power will be in the hands of those who have no hunger for power, but who are, rather, dedicated to the cause of all humanity. There will be ample leisure for recreation. . . . Leisure, and no further waste of natural resources. Cities will be planned, and clean; power will be drawn from the atom, and food from the sea. The land will recover its topsoil. The life span of the human being will be increased. . . . Money too may have vanished. The state will receive what is made and give what is needed. Imagine this continent—the great cities things of beauty; squalor gone; the rivers conserved; the beauty of the landscape, conserved. No longer suffering but beauty will be worshipped. Art will mirror no longer struggle but fulfillment. Each man will know himself—without delusions, without muddle, and within the limits of that self-knowledge will construct a sane and useful life. Work and love: parks; orchards. Understand me. The factors which for ages have warped the mind of man and stunted his body will be destroyed; man will grow like a tree in the open. There will be no waste. No pain and above all no *waste*. And this heaven will come to this earth, and come soon. (75)

In a similar way, the personal dedication of each man is markedly unmatched. It is not the traditionally religious man who is the zealot. Hook occupies himself, as will the aged, reminiscing, recalling the "better" things of the past: better carpentry and building materials, better people, hard work which kept men from idleness. He regrets his sins and mistakes but feels he has asked forgiveness and is waiting patiently for death and eternal rest. While he waits he brings little words of comfort to his aging friends and "believes." At the end of each day he reads his Bible, "its spine in shreds" (121), and goes to sleep peacefully.

Conner's dedication, on the other hand, is a burning flame within him. He has no peace. He has no patience with poverty, illness, superstition, or "belief" without reason. Early in the story he says to one of the elderly men, "I want to help these men to hold up their heads; to retain to the end the dignity that properly belongs to every member, big or little, of humanity" (16). At another point the narrator says of him, "Conner wanted things *clean*; the world needed renewal" (46), and describes him as "young for the importance of his position, devout in the service of humanity" (12), and again as "a man dedicated to a dynamic vision: that of Man living healthy and unafraid beneath blank skies" (47). Toward the end of the story, after failure for the idealistic young man is spelled out in a stoning by the elderly inmates, Conner still believes in himself; "he prized a useful over a pleasant life. Wherever I can serve, he told himself" (108). The author may be suggesting that the reason for Conner's failure lies in his belief that he is self-sufficient, that he needs no strength but his own: "Within he stubbornly retained . . . the conviction that he was the hope of the world" (109).

In somewhat the same proportion, the arguments between the two men regarding the existence of God are significantly unbalanced. Hook uses small evidences from life to explain the source of his faith and, in his calm acceptance and simple belief, waits quietly for life to win his debate for him. Conner makes elaborate speeches, his arguments reasonable, intelligent, impressive. The narrator introduces us to Conner's disbelief in his first description of the poorhouse director:

Conner thought of no one as God. The slats of light from
the east and south windows, broken into code by the leaves
and stems of the plants on the sills, spoke no language to
him. He had lost all sense of omen. Rising as early as Hook,
he had looked at the same sky and seen nothing but promise
of a faultless day for the fair. . . . Beyond . . . hung the
white walls of the universe, the listless, permissive mother for
whom Conner felt not a shred of awe. (12–13)

A discussion on a rainy afternoon between the direc-
tor and the inmate brings the two to open debate about
God and creation. Conner goes to battle to destroy
Hook's faith.

"What makes you think, God exists?" As soon as he pro-
nounced the ominous hollow noun, Conner knew absolutely
he could drive the argument down to the core of shame that
lay heavily in any believer's heart.

"Why, there are sever-al sorts of evidence," Hook said, as
he held up one finger then added a second, "there is what of
Cre-ation I can see, and there are the inner spokesmen."

"Creation. Look at the smoke of your cigar; twisting, ex-
panding, fading. That's the shape of Creation. You've seen
. . . photographs of nebulae: smears of smoke billions of
miles wide. What do you make of their creation?"

"I know little of astronomy. Now a flower's creation—"

"Is also an accident."

"An ac-cident?" Hook smiled softly and he touched the
fingertips together, better to give his attention.

"Lightning stirred certain acids present on the raw earth.
Eventually the protein molecule occurred, and in another
half-billion years the virus, and from then on its evolution.
Imagine a blind giant tossing rocks through eternity. At some
point he would build a cathedral."

"It seems implaus-ible."

"It's mathematics. The amounts of time it takes is the
factor that seems implausible. But the universe has endless
time."

. . . "I do not quite see how any amount of time can gen-
erate something from nothing."

"Presumably there was always something. Though relatively, very little. The chief characteristic of the universe is, I would say, emptiness. There is infinitely more nothing in the universe than anything else."

"Indeed, you propose to extinguish re-ligion by measuring quantities of nothing. Now why should no matter how much nothing be imposing, when my little fingernail, by being something, is of more account?"

"Yes, but there is something. Stars; many of such size that were one placed in the position of the sun we would be engulfed in flame. The issue is, can any sane mind believe that a young carpenter in Syria two thousand years ago *made* those monstrous balls of gas?" (78–79)

One is prepared at this point for the debate to end in favor of the logical, highly articulate Conner, but it is not over. There is no winning an argument against a man who has Hook's faith. He replies, even changing the subject slightly if necessary, but he always replies with confidence. His is a *knowing*, not an arguing belief. As the discussion continues, Conner tells us that "if the universe was made, it was made by an idiot" and that "Life is a maniac in a closed room" (79–80). Hook, not the least unsettled by the young man's frightful interpretations, tells how the very factors which arouse fear in the nonbeliever give the faithful confidence and comfort.

"Now it has never been claimed," Hook said, "that the Creator's mind is a book open for all to read. This I do know, that that part of the uni-verse which is visible to me, as distinct from that which is related to me, is an unfailing source of consolation. . . . As to the stars which so repel you, they are to me points of light arranged at random, to give the night sky adorn-ment. I have sometimes thought, had you and your kind arranged the stars, you would have set them geometrically, or had them spell a thought-provoking sentence." (80)

Not recognizing the older man's inner peace in replies like this one, Conner, at all times during the argument, is certain that Hook is defeated. He is so sure of himself that he is sure he knows the innermost thoughts of his opponent, no matter what Hook's words imply. He continues to "prove" that there is no soul, only glands, water, nerves. He believes that he has proved that there is no God and that the universe is an ominous accident.

The debate over, the elderly Hook, who by all appearances should be defeated, has the last word, and the reader hears not only Hook but Updike's grandfather, and John Updike himself, voicing the theme of *The Poorhouse Fair*:

There is no goodness, without belief. There is nothing but busy-ness. And if you have not believed, at the end of your life you shall know you have buried your talent in the ground of this world and have nothing saved, to take to the next. (81)

David Galloway, who believes that Updike "despises the simple, unthinking handmaid of church or state" [4] would not agree, but we need little more to assure us that the author's sympathies are more clearly with Hook than with Conner. There are, however, still more clues. Even though the narrator is not necessarily the author, in this case Updike has identified Hook as his own grandfather. It seems safe to seek the author's opinions in the narrator's words. Toward the end of the story, the narrator says, "We grow backward, aging into our father's opinions and even into those of our grandfathers" (112). At various points in the account he reveals the utmost respect, even reverence for the Christian doctrine and for the Bible. He calls the Gospels "those springs of no certain bottom, which you never find dry" (121). Even speaking through Conner, he describes Christianity as a "venerable faith" (81).

It would be simple at this point to conclude that Updike is traditionally Christian, believing in his grandfather's God the Father as Creator of the universe and personal acquaintance, believing in eternal life in a heaven too awesome to describe. The truth is not that simple. The student of Updike must consider the respectful hearing the author has given both the Christian and the humanistic points of view. He must also admit that paradoxically, Conner, representing godlessness, achieves a moral victory in his defeat at the hands of "Christian" stupidity and intolerance. And yet it is Hook who is undefeated and strong even as the moment of death approaches.

Two philosophies have been given a hearing and, for all their impressiveness, found lacking. The ideal humanist, Conner, needs something more than self and a perfect welfare state, glitteringly successful as they might become. Hook, the faithful Christian, has allowed his thinking to stop in order to keep his faith. He, too, needs to reexamine his religion, which has not kept up with society's progress. Christianity does not meet the needs of the new age.

The author seems to suggest that the missing ingredient could be found in the religious point of view, but he does not lead us to it. Significantly, the book ends with a troubled and questioning old man. Hook climbs, perhaps symbolically, "the stairs, the 'wooden hill'" (121), toward sleep, death, and his Heaven, but he is not at peace. There is unrest in his waiting hours as there is indecision in the thoughts of his artistic creator. The young Conner has disturbed Hook. The old man wants to console the young man, to cool his fire, to atone for the intolerance of his own feeble peers, but he does not know what it is he must say to Conner. He knows there is something still lacking in his own formula. He has admitted failures of his generation, recognized the practical goodness of Conner's. He feels "right with God," but he wonders what is missing—what it is he needs to help young Conner. "He stood motionless, half in moonlight, groping after the fitful shadow of advice he must impart to Conner, as a bond between them and a testament to endure his dying in the world" (127).

Through the final sentence in the novel, Updike reveals his conclusion: The answer has not been found; the search must go on. Hook asks, "What was it?" (127). The story ends. The author's search continues.

4

Rabbit, Run

The search for a religion to fit the needs of modern man continues in Updike's second novel, *Rabbit, Run*. The leading character, Harry "Rabbit" Angstrom, a grotesque innocent who seeks "something that wants [him] to find it" (107), represents another attempt to show that man needs some undefined element which modern American culture—specifically twentieth-century Christianity, small Pennsylvania town version—has not provided. Updike tells the story of the misdirected and uncharted search of an earnest but immature social misfit, attempting to show that man intuitively desires "something" which is missing from our modern culture. In *The Poorhouse Fair* the author contrasts the inadequacies of rational intellectualism with those of traditional Christianity. The search for a compromise—an intellectual and spiritual coupling of Christian faith and humanistic reasoning—is Updike's own. In *Rabbit, Run* he transfers the search to one of his characters, Harry Angstrom, and the dimensions of the quest become entirely new. Rabbit searches without knowing what it is he seeks. Something beyond his own weak will draws him, impels him to search. The author seems to be telling us that "the search is the thing," that instinct or intuition demands that we search. Or perhaps he is saying that anyone, whether he be intellectual or faithful or immoral and simple can sense the reality of God. Perhaps he is saying that God tries to reach us.

At various moments in the story, Rabbit, the moral

derelict, seems on the verge of some kind of discovery about the channels through which he should search. They are, significantly, often related to the Church, Christian doctrine, or Christian love. Paradoxically, the very things which might be expected to guide him, however, seem to mislead him. And one paradox suggests another.

The principal paradox in the story is that of the value of human personality. In his sympathetic and open-minded portrayal of Rabbit, the author seems to be defining the uniqueness of the individual and at the same time suggesting that if we allow the individual his unique inheritance, he will fail as a member of society. There can be no conformity in uniqueness. Without conformity, society as we know it, fails.

At the end of the novel, as at the close of *The Poorhouse Fair*, we discover that there is no solution to the paradox unless it is the search itself. In a kind of tragic optimism, Rabbit, a complete failure in the world his culture has created for him, continues in his persistent search for self-realization. Herein, the uniqueness of human personality is defended, but the problem of the individual in society remains unsolved. The search for an unknown element which can unify the good but divergent aspects of our culture is continued.

Rabbit, Run is much more complex than a casual first reading is likely to suggest. It is an account of one man's escape from the restrictions of social conformity and at the same time a report of his urgent pursuit of "something" which even the desperate searcher cannot define. It is an account of release and yet of lonely despair. It is a story of search for some kind of religious meaning to fit the needs of individuals in contemporary society which negates individualism. It is a search for something Christianity seems to have touched upon but which many who consider themselves Christian have not recognized. It is the simple Rabbit Angstrom's search, and it is the search of his complex creator, John Updike. It is the search for that essence which impels us to search.

Rabbit's searching seems to be spurred by two things, Christian instruction and intuition. The intuitive search has much stronger impetus than the learned, but both must be examined if one wishes to understand the conflicting drives of the young man's psyche and the theme of the book.

Rabbit's Christian training, though it has little effect on his morals, clearly influences his thinking and, again, paradoxically, is partly the cause of his irrational behavior. Realizing that he is not living up to expectations of a nominally Christian society, he nevertheless considers himself Christian. In a scene perfectly geared to his level of maturity, Rabbit is watching the Mouseketeers on television. Jimmy, one of the performers, appears and solemnly pronounces the lesson of the day.

Rabbit watches him attentively; he respects him. . . .
"Know Thyself, a wise old Greek once said. Know Thyself.
Now what does that mean, boys and girls? It means, be what
you are. Don't try to be Sally or Johnny or Fred next door; be
yourself. God doesn't want a tree to be a waterfall, or a flower
to be a stone. God gives to each one of us a special talent."
Janice and Rabbit become unnaturally still; both are Christians. God's name makes them feel guilty. (12)

Rabbit, like an obedient child, listens to an "authoritative" voice of modern society as he has doubtless listened to his Sunday school teacher throughout childhood. He is naïve and vulnerable. He will remember the Mouseketeer's instruction and make an effort to know himself even if it means ignoring his responsibilities to his family. He has also listened dutifully to the Christian teachings, and, within his level of understanding, makes them a part of his limited but sincere philosophy of self-fulfillment.

Correspondingly, Rabbit has a limited understanding of sin, but he does have a strong awareness of wrong-doing, and he does have feelings of guilt. Passing the bars and clubs on the street at night, he is almost frightened, associating alcohol and cards with a "depressing kind of sin" (18). Earlier in the account he had felt the newness of a clean March morning and had dedicated himself with a child-like impulse to a fresh beginning by throwing away a full package of cigarettes.

When, after having deserted his wife, Janice, he returns to her on the night of the birth of their second child, he is intensely aware of his wrong-doing. "He is certain that as a consequence of his sin Janice or the baby will die. His sin a conglomerate of flight, cruelty, obscenity, and conceit; a black clot embodied in the entrails of the birth" (164).

His consciousness of sin has little effect on his conduct, however. Lying in bed with Ruth, a prostitute, Rabbit puts into practice one of his Christian lessons; he prays. We are aware that his prayer isn't going to change his way of living, but we learn that it comforts and reassures him, allowing him to ignore responsibility. The scene is not only a revelation of Rabbit's shallowness but is also a subtle comment on the value of some of the Church's most precious practices.

Church bells ring loudly. He moves to her side of the bed to watch the crisply dressed people go into the limestone church across the street, whose lit window had lulled him to sleep. He reaches and pulls up the shade a few feet. The rose window is dark now. . . . The thought of these people having the bold idea of leaving their homes to come here and pray pleases and reassures Rabbit, and moves him to close his own eyes and bow his head with a movement so tiny Ruth won't notice. *Help me, Christ. Forgive me. Take me down the way. Bless Ruth, Janice, Nelson, my mother and father, Mr. and Mrs. Springer, and the unborn baby. Forgive Tothero and all the others. Amen.* (77)

His prayers as dutifully said as those of a little child murmuring "Now I lay me down to sleep," Rabbit accepts the comforts of his pillow and of his prostitute's body.

Giving up cigarettes, feeling sinful, praying, and loving the sight of the church are not the only evidences of Rabbit's Christian orientation. After deserting his wife, he allows himself to be picked up by Eccles, the rector of the Episcopal church, and listens to the minister's admonitions as a child might listen to his father. Knowing Eccles' purpose, Rabbit does not escape in fear of being coaxed back to his wife; instead he pursues the cleric's friendship. It comforts him and gives him a feeling of sanctity as does attendance at church. After returning to his wife for a short time, Rabbit goes to church and believes he has been excused for all his faults.

Harry is happy to go to Eccles' church. Not merely out of affection for Eccles, though there's that; but because he considers himself happy, lucky, blessed, forgiven, and wants to give thanks. (195)

But there are attractions stronger than those of the minister's friendship and the church's sanctified atmosphere, and with the slightest upset in his home life, Rabbit leaves again. Janice resorts to alcohol for consolation. In a drunken state, she tries to bathe the new baby and drowns her in the tub. Rabbit is summoned by Eccles and returns, again keenly aware of his guilt.

He expects never to go to sleep and, awaking with the slant of sunshine and the noise of doors slamming downstairs, feels his body has betrayed his soul. He dresses in haste, more panicked now than at any time yesterday. The event is realer. Invisible cushions press against his throat and slow his legs and arms; the kink in his chest has grown thick and crusty. *Forgive me, forgive me,* he keeps saying silently to no one. . . . Janice is awake. . . . He . . . lies down on the bed beside her. . . . She tells him, "I can't stand to look at anyone except you. I can't bear to look at the others."

"It wasn't your fault," he tells her. "It was mine." (231)

This time the prayers and ceremonies of the Church do not comfort him. Eccles is busy with other members of the family and can devote little time to him, and Rabbit experiences fear and loneliness which reveal the quality in his character which drives him with greater force than his Christian lessons toward his undefined "something that wants me to find it." Eccles has tried to convince him that his conduct is more important than his vague search. The cleric has told him that "Christianity isn't looking for a rainbow. If it were what you think it is we'd pass out opium at services. We're trying to *serve* God, not *be* God" (112).

But Rabbit's intuitive drive for self-realization continues to plague him. After the baby's death he asks,

"What shall I do?"

Eccles glances up nervously. He is very tired; Harry has never seen him look so tired. . . . "Do what you are doing," he says. "Be a good husband. A good father. Love what you have left."

"And that's enough?"

"You mean to earn forgiveness? I'm sure it is, carried out through a lifetime."

"I mean"—He's never before felt *pleading* with Eccles— "remember that thing we used to talk about? The thing behind everything."

"Harry, you know I don't think that thing exists in the way you think it does." (233-34)

But Harry does believe it, and the drive to find "it" is much stronger than the guilt he has felt or his love for his living child, Nelson, his wife, the Church, or for acceptance by his community. He deserts them all at the graveside ceremony and runs.

The reader is not surprised, for he has been prepared

for such conduct since his introduction to Rabbit early in the story. Throughout, the evidence that Rabbit will follow his intuition and not Christian guidance is repeated.

On a twilight walk he "now and then touches with his hand the rough bark of a tree or the dry twigs of a hedge, to give himself the small answer of a texture" (17), and we know that he questions. We see his perpetual search in his vague love for the sky and for climbing to the tops of mountains. Without knowing why, "he wants to believe in the sky as the source of all things" (233). He takes Ruth to the top of Mt. Judge in an effort to find a companion in his vague search, but she does not comprehend. He knows there is something to look for though he cannot define it.

O.K. He brought them up here. To see what? . . . The city is huge in the middle view, and he opens his lips as if to force the lips of his soul to receive the taste of truth about it, as if truth were a secret in such low solution that only immensity can give us a sensible taste. (95–96)

His search for truth is not a pretense or a way to avoid responsibility. He honestly believes that "somewhere there is something better for him" (225) and that he not only has a right to refuse to conform but a duty to do so. Conformity would mean abandoning his search. Eccles, in one of his first encounters with Rabbit, learns of the young man's sincerity. He asks the runaway husband,

"Do you believe in God?"

Rabbit answers promptly, "Yes."

Eccles blinks in surprise. . . . "Do you think, then, that God wants you to make your wife suffer?"

"Let me ask you. Do you think God wants a waterfall to be a tree?" This question of Jimmy's [the Mouseketeer] sounds, Rabbit realizes, ridiculous. . . .

"No," Eccles says after thought. "But I think He wants a little tree to become a big tree."

"If you're telling me I'm not mature, that's one thing I don't cry over since as far as I can make out it's the same thing as being dead." (90)

We find further evidence of his confidence in himself through a conversation he has with Ruth. He feels that he wants nothing of maturity as society defines it and that, furthermore, others have faith in him as he is.

"Oh, all the world loves you," Ruth says suddenly. "What I wonder is why?"

"I'm lovable," he says.

"I mean why the hell *you*. What's so special about *you?*"

"I'm a mystic," he says. "I give people faith." (121)

Rabbit has heard this half serious explanation from Eccles, decided it is true, and accepted it seriously. His sense of his own importance is repeatedly evident. After one of his afternoons of wandering alone and trying to decide what it is he is looking for, we learn that "nowhere did an opinion tally with his own, that Harry Angstrom was worth saving and could be saved" (140).

The idea that he needs "saving" comes, of course, from his Christian orientation, but his method of redemption through doing as he pleases implies that intuition has the stronger voice. "Being oneself" means to him "doing as one feels like doing," and he is so thoroughly imbued with the idea that he feels others respect him for it. In a conversation with Ruth he says, "If you have the guts to be yourself . . . other people'll pay your price" (125).

Of course Rabbit, too, must pay a price. Rejecting society, he is in turn rejected, and he must, if he is to have any integrity, constantly seek some nebulous essence which he cannot even define. Lucidly demonstrative of his undefined search is a scene with Eccles on the golf course. They have discussed Rabbit's conduct, which the minister sees as "monstrously selfish" (112), but which Rabbit feels is justified in his effort to be true to himself. Eccles cannot accept Rabbit's reasoning. The author explains it in the metaphor of a golf ball's flight:

His ball is hung way out, lunarly pale against the beautiful black blue of storm clouds. . . . It recedes along a line straight as a ruler-edge. Stricken; sphere, star, speck. It hesitates, and Rabbit thinks it will die, but he's fooled, for the ball makes this hesitation the ground of a final leap: with a kind of visible sob takes a last bite of space before vanishing in falling. "That's it!" he cries and, turning to Eccles with a smile of aggrandizement, repeats, "That's it." (112–13)

Rabbit is something sent into the world on an impetus not his own, but he has a significance which is his own. Having reached an awareness of his singular significance, he must decide between society's plan for his life on the one hand, and freedom to follow his intuitive drives on the other. He chooses to follow intuition, a course which he feels is a sacred responsibility. He knows the cost of the freedom he has chosen. The ball has chosen its course, vanished, and fallen.

The clues the reader finds as to the meaning of Rabbit's search are sifted from this story one at a time and are found to resemble those in Updike's poetry and his first novel, *The Poorhouse Fair*. The search is an almost instinctive thing. Man's Maker, whatever He is, gives even the most unimpressive individual a drive to search for the significance of his uniqueness. Society does not permit an unhampered search. The Christian Church, a part of that society, not only fails to guide the twentieth-century searcher, it sometimes misleads him, and yet it offers the most promising area of search.

Again and again Rabbit seems nearest his goal when he reflects on the activities of Christian people or when he studies a Church symbol.

He hates all the people on the street in dirty everyday clothes, advertising their belief that the world arches over a pit, that death is final, that the wandering thread of his feelings leads nowhere. Correspondingly he loves the ones dressed for church; the pressed business suits of portly men give substance and respectability to his furtive sensations of the invisible. . . . He is surrounded by people who know God; he has come into a field of flowers. (196)

His "wandering thread of feeling" leads him still again to Christianity as a channel for his search. At the moment of his first complete break with conformity, his first encounter with Ruth, Rabbit turns to a church window which becomes a symbol of his intuitive (not learned) hope.

There is only the church across the way, gray, somber, confident. Lights behind its rose window are left burning, and this circle of red and purple and gold seems in the city night *a hole punched in reality to show the abstract brilliance burning underneath.* [Italics mine] (69)

It is not *in* the Church but *through* it, perhaps beyond it that one will find an "abstract brilliance," something better than the city's reality or the Church's traditional promise. Rabbit vaguely *feels* the direction he must take; he does not understand it.

The same window looks out over the street in the last episode of the story. Rabbit is walking away from the "reality" of his responsibilities in the city. This time he only "remembers what once consoled him by seeming to make a hole where he looked through into underlying brightness, and lifts his eyes to the church window . . . a dark circle in a stone facade" (254).

The "dark circle" gives no new impressions. He has given up all guidance other than intuition. He has made his decision: he will accept rejection and will continue his lonely search. As he strides from block to gray block, something in the dismal scene and in his decision "makes him happy" (255). In the midst of apparent hopelessness, the reader feels, as he has in other Updike works, a sudden unreasonable but optimistic lift. It is the fact that one must search that is hopeful. Rabbit searches because he can't do otherwise; man searches because he is impelled to. Somewhere through his church windows or beyond them is an "abstract brightness" which, if he ever finds it, will answer his need and reveal his Motivator.

5

The Centaur

John Updike's third novel, *The Centaur*, 1963, won the 1964 *National Book Award for Fiction* and elicited critical judgments ranging from Richard Gilman's "a pastiche, a sly exercise, a piece of bravado, an evasion"[1] to David Galloway's "[a novel which] illustrates the far-reaching significance of the modern saint's apparently solipistic [*sic*] experience."[2] Seen in the company of his other fiction and poetry, *The Centaur* appears to be a part of Updike's search for new dimensions in religion which will satisfy the needs of the neoteric individual. As in much of the poetry and in *Rabbit, Run*, it stresses the confusion of our time, especially for the dedicated seeker after Truth. It elaborates on man's perplexity by presenting him as half beast, half god; half bad, half good. Like *The Poorhouse Fair*, it points up inadequacies of phases of our social structure, this time adding the educational system to the list of criticized institutions. With greater conviction than that of earlier novels, *The Centaur* declares God's existence and, with optimism characteristic of the author at this point in his writing career, sees hope in the perpetual cycles of life and death. Man is only a part of God's vast plan, only a breath in the timeless life of all things, but he is significant. Each breath is necessary to the Omnipresent Life, even if, as in this case, it completes only an ubiquitous sigh.

In *The Centaur* Updike continues the search for evidence that what he believes is man's inherent goodness, though sometimes barely discernible in the complexity of his makeup, coupled with his yearning to find his place in the order of all things, is proof that God exists. He continues to search for a philosophy and a code of living to accommodate the needs and hopes of the modern seeker.

The confusion metaphorically described in the Updike poems "Bendix" and "Reel" is exemplified in the life of George Caldwell, tragic hero of *The Centaur*. Unlike Harry Angstrom of *Rabbit, Run*, who evades responsibility to search for Truth, George Caldwell, a high school teacher, drives himself mercilessly in dedicated service to his profession, the community, and his family. Service is his way of life, his way of searching for his place in the cosmic design. Devoting himself to his pupils is a sacred duty; searching for Truth is his second nature. But failure is Caldwell's most familiar experience.

His own perplexity about his role in life creates the framework for his failure. He fails to discipline his pupils adequately; he fails in his communications with his wife and in meeting the everyday needs of his son. He believes he has wasted his life in a profession for which he is unsuited, and he submits to frustration and to the jibes of pompous, empty-headed challengers as if he were a giant conquered by pygmies. He accepts the role of the born loser, tormenting himself with his inability to find answers for philosophic questions most people don't bother to ask. The poet's words that "We whirl, or seem to whirl, / Or seem to seem to; whorls / Within more whorls unfurl / In matters, habits, morals" describe the experience of Caldwell. He cannot find a code of living which will incorporate his ideal of service with society's concept of success.

He cannot understand why failure should be his lot and does not realize that his life of service and love place him in the role of a rough-hewn saint. What he has taught his students by example, by love and sacrifice, far outweighs the value of "facts" they might have missed in his lectures. Devoting himself completely to others and to the pursuit of Truth, he fails only superficially, only by temporal standards. Selflessly he serves his profession, his pupils, his son, his wife—even the worthless tramp on the street to whom he would give his coat or his purse. If Christian standards are a criterion, he is successful: he lives by the law of love. By the standards of modern society he is a gawky misfit. In his own eyes he is hopelessly inadequate as husband, father, teacher, and learner.

One of the reasons for Caldwell's mental turmoil is the fact that his companions in a nominally Christian society do not live by the laws of love. He is unique and alone. Another is that religion as it is practiced in the organized Church does not satisfy his needs. A scene in the gymnasium at the high school illustrates the Church's failure toward people like the devoted teacher and confused searcher. The Reverend March, minister of a Protestant church, has been introduced through a conversation with one of the women teachers. Caldwell, depressed and anxious about his own possibly imminent death, approaches the minister.

"I hope I'm not interrupting you and Vera here; the fact is I'm badly troubled in my mind."

With a nervous glance at Vera, who has turned her head and might slip from his side, March asks, "Oh. What about?"

"Everything. The works. I can't make it add up and I'd be grateful for your viewpoint."

Now March's glance travels everywhere but into the face opposite him as he looks through the crowd for some rescue from this tousled tall maniac. "Our viewpoint does not essentially differ from the Lutheran," he says. "It's my hope that someday all the children of the Reformation will be reunited." (251–52)

There follows a fruitless discussion about the differences between the Presbyterian and the Orthodox Calvinistic beliefs, none of which is really what Caldwell wishes to talk about, but all of which is his awkward way of getting into topics he hopes to discuss. The minister, however, does not wish to be bothered. He feels that as long as he is popular with his congregation he does not need to serve the doubting questioner whom Caldwell represents. Besides, he has other things on his mind.

March's gray eyes are exploding with pain and irritation as the danger of Vera's leaving him grows. "This is burlesque!" he shouts. "A basketball game is no place to discuss such matters. Why don't you come and visit me in my study sometime, Mr. ———?"

"Caldwell. George Caldwell. Vera here knows me."

Vera turns back with a wide smile. "Somebody invoke my name? I don't understand a thing about theology."

"Our discussion of it has just been concluded," Reverend March tells her. (253)

Wherewith he dismisses Caldwell to return to a more entertaining pastime. In an earlier scene the author has revealed the true character of this minister of the Christian Church. March has been subtly flirtatious with the sensuous Vera, who asks him what he is doing at the basketball game.

"I came," he answers, "to shepherd forty pagan brutes from Sunday school. . . ."

She laughs. "But why?"

"Why does anything like this happen to me?" he sternly asks, slightly pop-eyed. "Why do all the ladies of my parish bake cupcakes once a month and sell them to each other? Why does the town drunk keep calling me on the telephone? Why do these people keep showing up in fancy hats on Sunday morning to hear me prattle about an old book?" Successful beyond his expectations, the warm swirl of her laughter lifting him deliciously, he goes on and on in this vein. . . . Though his faith is intact and is infrangible as metal, it is also like metal dead. . . . He mocks it." (236–37)

Caldwell needs something more than this self-satisfied role-player to lead him in his search. He needs something more than the "dead" faith of hypocrisy. His questions about the meaning of life and death are honest. His need is urgent. The representative of the Church is not only incapable of understanding the desperate man but is also unwilling to help him.

The criticism of the Church implied in this passage is similar to that found elsewhere in Updike's fiction, but for the first time the American educational system also comes under attack. Updike does not criticize technical or academic functions of the schools, but he does suggest that a close look be taken at the moral and professional standards of their personnel. The setting of *The Centaur* is primarily a high school building and its locale; its characters are teachers and administrators and pupils. In addition to being an account of three days in the life of school teacher George Caldwell, the book is a commentary on the misguided, undisciplined pupils and their inadequate leaders. Updike exposes the morals and motives of a few of those who should be character models for the young, and he paints a vivid if ugly picture of a modern American classroom.

The first paragraph in the book describes an almost unbelievable situation in which the teacher, Caldwell, has just been hit in the ankle by an arrow which has pierced the flesh.

Caldwell turned and as he turned his ankle received an arrow. The class burst into laughter. The pain scaled the slender core of his shin, whirled in the complexities of his knee, and, swollen broader, more thunderous, mounted into his bowels. . . . The laughter of the class, graduating from the first shrill bark of surprise into a deliberately aimed hooting, seemed to crowd against him. . . . Several of the boys in their bright shirts all colors of the rainbow had risen upright at their desks, leering and baying at their teacher, cocking their muddy shoes on the folding seats. The confusion became unbearable. (3–4)

Wondering if the author is really serious, the reader hurries on, hoping that the school teacher will wake soon and be released from his nightmare. The nightmare continues.

Another classroom scene, which is also written partly in metaphor so that one does not know where reality leaves off and symbol begins, is just as subjectively critical. Knowing it is not a literal description of a modern classroom, the reader is nevertheless repulsed at the scene, which depicts the conduct and the thoughts of administrator, teacher, and students in the school. The teacher, Caldwell, struggles under a painful handicap while lecturing to a roomful of insolent, sensual young people who hear very little of his remarkable account of the creation of the universe. The principal, an administrative tyrant and a lecherous old man, sits in the room ogling the breasts of a young girl and taking notes on the quality of Caldwell's teaching. The pupils pop bubble gum, dump biology laboratory specimens on the floor, tickle each other with pencils, and make rude remarks. The confusion increases until chaos is complete. The teacher fails as a disciplinarian; the students are barbarian; the principal is lascivious. The author's message is clear.

Revealing the weakness as well as the strength of Caldwell, Updike presents an unbiased, sympathetic portrait of a devoted but misplaced man. Caldwell is helpless and inadequate, caught up in a profession for which he is temperamentally ill fitted and in economic circumstances which give him no choice but to continue. He charges day after day through a calendar of conflicts. Telling the story of his failure, Updike tells of the failure of thousands like him in American schools.

Man's confusion in this life is brought about by things

other than his faulty social institutions, however. Man is basically a creature of both animal and godlike characteristics. He is half bad, half good; half beast, half god. This philosophy is illustrated through extensive metaphor which makes the author's point almost too well. George Caldwell is an Olinger high school teacher and the sacrificing father of Peter, but he is also Chiron, the mythical centaur who taught the young and gave up his immortality for Prometheus. Like Chiron, Caldwell has godlike qualities and mortal weaknesses. The reader is distracted from the story and its meaning by an often overstrained metaphor. As the book opens, Chiron and Caldwell are given about equal attention. As the story progresses, one is relieved of the artificiality of the literary device and carried into the stream of events of Caldwell's life only to be forcefully reminded, periodically, that the metaphor is still in use and that he should keep Chiron's story in mind as he proceeds. A device intended to refine the reader's understanding actually distracts because of its exaggerated use, but its purpose in *The Centaur* is obvious. Man's perplexity about his rightful place in the cosmic structure rises from the fact that he is a complex creature neither god nor beast yet resembling both.

This duality of temperament and character is not limited to the role of Caldwell but is demonstrated in almost every person portrayed. Caldwell's wife is, on the one hand, unequivocally dedicated to nature and the land and on the other singularly selfish in her way of life, which adds to the difficulties of Caldwell's existence. Peter, their son, both seeks understanding of life and is a self-pitying and undisciplined teen-ager. Vera, who seems to Peter to be warm and motherly, is to others the embodiment of sensuality. The high school students who at one time torment their teacher are at another wistful young people who respect and love him.

Caldwell, of course, is the chief example of complexity.

He deeply loves people, even when they are completely undeserving of his devotion. He is conscientious and thoughtful, devoted and long-suffering. He is also awkward, incompetent, self-effacing, and prone to failure and accident. Vera, as Venus, in a symbolic scene in the women's locker room at the high school, speaks of Chiron (Caldwell) as "a creature combining the refinement and consideration of a man with . . . the massive potency of a stallion" (24).

To his son, Peter, Caldwell is too complex to understand. At one time the boy recalls, "Once I had stood beside his knees on the brick walk leading to the grape arbor of our house in Olinger and felt him look level into the tops of the horsechestnut trees and believed that nothing could ever go wrong as long as we stood so" (65). As a teen-ager, Peter sees his father in a different light, "his face, compounded of shiny lumps and sallow slack folds . . . seemed both tender and brutal, wise and unseeing" (64–65). To all who love him, Caldwell is an enigma. He is Updike's centaur—creature somewhere between god and beast—man complex and confused.

The reader finds in *The Centaur*, as in Updike's other early novels and in his poetry, a glimmer of optimism. The story of a luckless school teacher who gives up and dies because he cannot cope with his own failure—and this seems more nearly the case than the more esthetic reason that he is Chiron dying for Prometheus—seems an unlikely situation for the subject of hope, but Updike makes it so. Throughout the book there are little songs of praise for the *goodness* in men's lives. Caldwell is by Christian definition a good man. He fails to meet society's expectations and his own, but he is almost a Christlike figure in his sacrificial love for others. Seeing him as one of the several saints in Updike's novels, David Galloway says, "In the intensity of his love Caldwell comes closer than any of Updike's other characters to something like a traditional concept of Christ." [3] Updike suggests through Caldwell that there is hope as long as his kind of goodness lives.

At one point in the story Caldwell assures his family that "I was brought up to believe, and I still believe it, that God made Man as the last best thing in His Creation" (63). The author seems to be saying that man lacks much, but he is God's creation. The good that lives in him, even in small measure, is what God put there. The fact that it is there should give us hope. Paul A. Doyle sees all of Updike's fiction as an elaboration of "The Problem of Goodness and the Search for the Good Man." [4] In *The Centaur* a good man has been found. The fact that society would consider him unsuccessful seems to matter little. Just before Caldwell dies, he accepts his failure that it may die with him. The goodness that was his will live on in the lives of those he has influenced. Updike's optimism and hope are expressed in some of Caldwell's final thoughts: "Only Goodness lives. But it does live!" (297).

The source of that goodness gives cause for even greater optimism. Updike expresses in *The Centaur* his certainty that God lives. Caldwell's life is evidence of God's presence. Like the evidence described in the poem "Fever," Caldwell's love for others in the face of life's setbacks is a *revelation* of God's certainty. It does not argue for God or prove Him. It makes Him apparent. This may be the most important point made in the book. The line from "Fever" which states that "God exists" could be used to state the theme of *The Centaur*.

A scene between Caldwell and Hester, the French teacher at the high school, gives the leading character an opportunity to express his belief just as his life has demonstrated it, by unpretentious example:

"Say it again," Caldwell asks.
"*Dieu—est—tres* [sic]—*fin*. It's the sentence I've lived by."

"God is very—very fine?"

"Oui. Very fine, *very* elegant, *very* slender, very exquisite. *Dieu est tres fin.*"

"That's right. He certainly is. He's a wonderful old gentleman. I don't know where the hell we'd be without him." (194)

Caldwell has not been without Him. God's indefinable excellence is reflected in him, faintly, perhaps, but certainly.

Updike's optimistic point of view, expressed in the belief that *goodness lives* and that *God exists*, is further demonstrated in his repeated references to eternal life. Some of the critics see this tendency as an emphasis on death rather than on life. Richard Gilman says of *The Centaur*, "It is a novel which gives the appearance of engaging death, or more precisely the immanent existence of death. . . ." [5] An exparte reading certainly does give such an impression. Caldwell is injured even before the opening sentence. The arrow in his ankle symbolically suggests a poisonous or deathly instrument. He is ill and discouraged and, throughout the story, makes emotional preparations for his own death, but there are other threads of thought even more significant.

Caldwell lectures to his class on the creation of the universe and of plant and animal life and, by analogy, suggests a scientific concept which supports a belief in immortality. Scaling down the time elements to hours and minutes and describing the development of life in terms the students can readily understand, he also telescopes into the analogy a philosophic concept that those who sacrifice themselves for others earn eternal life. The certainty of death is, necessarily, certainty of life everlasting. Caldwell's emphasis on death—and Updike's—is converted to emphasis on life, eternal life, for all of God's creatures.

Amoebas never die; and those male sperm cells which enjoy success become the cornerstone of new life that continues beyond the father. But the volvox . . . by pioneering this new idea of cooperation, rolled life into the kingdom of certain—as opposed to accidental—death . . . while each cell is potentially immortal, by volunteering for a specialized function within an organized society of cells, it enters a compromised environment. The strain eventually wears it out and kills it. It dies sacrificially, for the good of the whole. These first cells who got tired of sitting around forever in a blue-green scum and said, "Let's get together and make a volvox," were the first altruists. The first do-gooders. If I had a hat on, I'd take it off to 'em. (42)

In the same vein he continues the story of the development of living creatures who die so that life may continue, endlessly. The final creature to appear in this category is man:

"One minute ago, flint-chipping, fire-kindling, death-foreseeing, a tragic animal appeared—" The buzzer rasped; halls rumbled throughout the vast building; faintness swooped at Caldwell but he held himself upright, having vowed to finish. "—called Man." (46)

The animal, man, is tragic because he knows he must die, individually, that his species may live eternally. These lines alone do not seem particularly optimistic as to man's role, but in the light of the rest of the book, they are. Caldwell sees all life as glorious; he is grateful for his own. He is not a wheel on which the universe turns, but he is part of the vast system. Like the tiny, lonely bird in "Mobile of Birds," he is significant. He finds joy in the fact that he has even limited significance. At one point, toward the end of the story, he contemplates the joy of living and even finds it possible to be grateful for death.

Wherever in the filth and confusion and misery, a soul felt joy, there the Lord came and claimed it as his own; . . . He thought of his wife's joy in the land and Pop Kramer's joy in the newspaper and his son's joy in the future [which he could inherit completely only upon his father's death] and was glad, grateful, that he was able to sustain these for yet a space more . . . he discovered that in giving his life to others he entered a total freedom. (296)

His joy and his life belong to "the Lord," to God. He belongs to God. His death is a part of the plan for *living forever as a part of God.*

Caldwell's concentration on the relationship between death and eternity does not eliminate him from those of Updike's characters who seek clarification of man's role in life, however. The search for purpose, for Truth, and for new religious concepts is woven into the texture of *The Centaur* as it is in much of Updike's fiction and poetry. George Caldwell believes in God, but he cannot answer all his own questions about man's relationship to Him. Caldwell is a Truth seeker. He does not hesitate to walk up to the minister, even in a crowded gymnasium, when he has a question to ask. His associates, too, see him as a searcher. Peter as narrator says of him, "My father brought to conversations a cavernous capacity for caring that dismayed strangers. They found themselves involved, willy-nilly, in a futile but urgent search for the truth" (82–83). Caldwell's physician, Doc Appleton, understands the emotional as well as the physical peculiarities of his patient. He says to Caldwell, "You're not a teacher, . . . You're a learner" (130). Caldwell indirectly acknowledges this characteristic in himself. He thanks a garage attendant for a simple statement about the hopeless condition of the family automobile. Whatever is the *truth* is worth knowing: "You've told me what you think is the truth and that's the greatest favor one man can do for another" (155).

A new significance is given to Updike's search in *The Centaur.* In this novel it is set apart by the use of a symbol highly appropriate to the twentieth-century search

and searcher. The story of Caldwell the teacher and
sacrificial father is paralleled with that of Chiron through
the symbol of the ancient mythical centaur, but the
modern Caldwell's search is carried on separately in the
highly contrasting and significantly modern symbol of
the automobile.

A painstaking study of Updike's symbolic use of the
automobile would probably offer new clues to interpretations of his works. The use of automobiles for purposes
other than transportation of characters is frequent in the
poetry, the novels, and the short stories. Maps that show
a mystifying complexity of roads from which man must
choose, roads that lead home again, service station at-
tendants who give sage advice, and automobiles that
provide love nests, security, deathbeds, and character
parallels occur again and again in Updike's work.

When Caldwell, a teacher in the 1960s, receives an
injury at the hands of a pupil, he does not go to a physician but to a competent auto mechanic for assistance.
Upon entering the garage where Caldwell hopes to find
help, he notices the "fragments of automobiles, fragile
and phantasmal, fenders like corpses of turtles, bristling
engines like disembodied hearts" (7–8), and the reader
gets his first clue to the significance of automobiles in
The Centaur. Automobiles have hearts. An injured man
seeks help at the hands of an auto mechanic. In the scene
that follows, Hummel, the mechanic, becomes physician;
the junior mechanics are technicians; the tools of their
trade are the physician's instruments. When Caldwell
smiles in embarrassment at his predicament, it is to them
"as if an automobile had tried to speak" (12). A man and
an automobile merge in identity.

Caldwell, trying to get his mind off the pain in his
ankle, brings his son into the metaphor: He recalls Peter
as a baby, "how he had pushed him on his Kiddy Kar
with a long forked stick along the pavements under the

horsechestnut trees. They had been too poor to afford a baby carriage; the kid had learned to steer, too early?" (12). Does this suggest the beginning of Peter's modern search? Peter, closely identified with his car, is pushed into life's paths before he has so much as a motor (and before he walks), but he learns to steer. Even the young child must begin to seek his own course in an age when conveyances go on their own power, steered by the lonely individual at the wheel.

As the scene progresses, the conversation turns from the repairs of Caldwell's ankle to those of his car. Hummel asks if the old '36 Buick he has sold his friend is "holding up," and Caldwell assures him that it is. It is more than just a car; it is a place where Caldwell and his son communicate. He tells Hummel, "It gives me a chance to talk to the kid. The kid and I hardly ever saw each other when we lived in town" (15). The Buick is also a source of personal pride. Caldwell says of its broken grill, "I kick myself every day for smashing up that grille" (16). Peter tells later of the pain his father suffered when the grille had been smashed, calls it the car's "grin," and says, "our car's face had jagged front teeth" (71). Caldwell, we soon learn, suffers from bad teeth. The battered condition of the car resembles that of its owner—not completely exhausted or useless but certainly deteriorating rapidly.

Caldwell's symbolic identity with his car is established, and his and his car's joint destiny is predicted in the first scene in Hummel's garage. To the alert reader the Buick readily becomes not only Caldwell's "other self" but his other corpse as well:

"That engine should be all right; the man never drove it over forty. He was an undertaker."

If Hummel had said that once, he had said it a thousand times. The fact seemed to fascinate him. "I'm not scared," Caldwell said, guessing that in Hummel's mind the car was full of ghosts. Actually, it was just an ordinary four-door sedan; there was no room to carry corpses. True, though, it was the blackest car Caldwell had ever seen. They really put the shellac on those old Buicks. (16)

As the story progresses, Caldwell's symptoms of illness increase, and breakdown of the Buick draws closer and closer. Toward the end of the first day of the three days covered in the story, the car stops running. Peter and his father try everything they can think of to persuade it to move. It refuses. Peter narrates the scene:

My father put his arms up on the wheel and lowered his head into them.
"Daddy?"
My father did not answer. The streetlight touched with a row of steady flecks the curve of his knit cap: the way Vermeer outlined a loaf of bread.
"What do you think's wrong?"
Now it occurred to me he had had an "attack" and the inexplicable behavior of the car was in fact an illusionistic reflection of some breakage in himself. I was about to touch him—I never touched my father—when he looked up with a smile of sorts on his bumpy and battered urchin's face. "This is the kind of thing," he said, "that's been happening to me all my life. I'm sorry you got involved in it. I don't know why the damn car doesn't move." (150)

But the reader sees the implication of the breakdown. The car is indeed an "illusionistic reflection of some breakage" in Caldwell. It does not move because, like its owner, it has weaknesses it cannot overcome of itself. Dependable as it always has been, it cannot go on forever. Because of its very nature, it will eventually wear out and die.

There are almost innumerable inferences that can be drawn regarding the meaning of the old automobile in this story. Whenever it appears, it does so in symbolic parallel with Caldwell. At the end of the second day of the account, it has been repaired and given a new lease on life. Caldwell, too, is somewhat renewed because he hears no bad news from his doctor, and he has had "repairs" at the dentist's office.

Then, for a second time when Caldwell tries to take Peter home at the end of the day, the Buick fails in its tasks. A hill which it has accomplished hundreds of times proves too much for the car and for Caldwell. Several times the Buick nearly reaches the top only to be backed down for another try and, finally, for a trip on level roads back to town. Caldwell and his car can no longer overcome the handicaps, the storms of life.

On the third day (and perhaps even the third day is symbolic), an effort is made again. This time the car makes it to within walking distance of the house. Peter is finally brought home out of danger. His father's failures have affected him, however, for he too is ill.

But Caldwell does not rest. Having given over his son to his mother's care and to recovery, he returns in the early hours of the next day to his half-buried Buick and to his search which is soon to end.

Now he came to the turn of the road. A hundred strides ahead of him he saw the Buick like a black mouth he must enter. It had been an undertaker's car. It made a black spot against the heaped snow. . . . As Chiron drew nearer, the shattered grille looked astonished. He saw now that this was the mouth of a tunnel he must crawl through. . . . A steep weariness mounted before him. . . . Drawing closer to the car, close enough to see an elongated distortion of himself in the fender, he understood. This was a chariot Zimmerman had sent for him. (297–98)

As Peter had seen his father's "illusionistic reflection" in the car, Caldwell now recognizes his own image. The Buick waits silently, half in its snowy grave, not to move on but to receive its other self. Caldwell understands. They will not continue on the worldly journey. A "chariot" is not for riding to school but for carrying its passenger to less finite destinations. The earthly journey is over.

Chiron came to the edge of limestone; his hoof scratched. A bit of pale pebble rattled into the abyss. He cast his eyes upward to the dome of blue and perceived that it was indeed a great step. Yes, in seriousness, a very great step, for which all the walking in his life had not prepared him. Not an easy step nor an easy journey, it would take an eternity to get there, an eternity as the anvil ever fell. . . . A little breeze met his face at the cliff-edge. His will, a perfect diamond under the pressure of absolute fear, uttered the final word. *Now* . . . . Chiron accepted death. (298–99)

Caldwell and his car have merged; now Chiron follows to complete the merging of identities ancient and modern. Caldwell is as ancient as the Greek god-animal creature, and he is as modern as a Buick. He is man, eternally living, dying, living again. In his modern version, he possesses, like an automobile, great power, but he cannot maneuver alone. He must have guidance. He does age and wear out. He will die that a younger, perhaps stronger man (or a new model) can continue the journey, the search.

If this were the end of the book, all the optimism seen in other aspects of the story would fade completely. The account does not end here, however. In an epilogue of a few lines the reader finds something ancient (older than Christianity), something mystical, something religious, something hopeful to take with him if he is a searcher. As in the poem "Zeppelin," the stars, permanent and certain but existing at an unfathomable distance, glitter in the heavens, eternally reminding us that there are answers. Chiron-Caldwell, now one of the stars, must have followed the right maps, confused as they were. He found no certain answers during his earthly journeys, but he never ceased searching. Now he is Sagittarius, himself both wise and unfathomable; he "assists in the regulation of our destinies," and offers eternal guidance to the few who, by his example, seek Truth.

Zeus had loved his old friend, and lifted him up, and set him among the stars as the constellation Sagittarius. Here, in the Zodiac, now above, now below the horizon, he assists in the regulation of our destinies, though in this latter time few living mortals cast their eyes respectfully toward Heaven, and fewer still sit as students to the stars. (299)

6

Of the Farm

Even without its epigraph from Sartre's existentialist writings, *Of the Farm* would easily be recognized as a novel illustrating a popular concept of personal freedom. The story touches on various other interpretations of freedom as well, but the one which receives the greatest attention is the common *distortion* of the existential doctrine suggesting that man is created by man, born a free agent, and responsible for what he makes of himself. "Responsible for what he makes of himself" becomes in this story what it does to many in modern society, "free to do whatever he pleases." It is a novel about people— very real people—who, disregarding the needs of those to whom they have the closest ties, do whatever they please and vaguely wonder why they have bad dreams. There are no devoted seekers after truth, no characters deeply concerned with the meaning of life, no philosophers questioning man's purpose. The book is about selfish, sensuous people who *exist*. The search which in the earlier novels gives leading characters purpose and direction and keeps them afloat above a hell of hopelessness is not present here. The fact that the author scrutinizes the lives of his characters, recognizes them for what they are, and exhibits them to us as he finds them is the only indication that the search in Updike's fiction for *good* or God for our times continues.

Of the Farm is also a transition novel. In some ways it relates to the first three of Updike's novels and earliest short stories; in some ways it is unique. It is a book about changes: changes in individuals and families and society; it is a book which reveals change in the author's course. It is one of those works which, to the critic with inadequate perspective, suggests a lapse of talents or even a total absence of creative purpose of the author. *Of the Farm*, taken out of context of the novels which precede it and the one which at present follows it, may leave one asking, "Now what in the world is this all about?" Understood in perspective, it becomes, like the perfectly conceived Updike sentence, a brief and perfectly conceived transition between chapters in the tome which will become the total work of an author who promises a new record in proliferation.

In literary transition we must have, first, something familiar to bridge the gap between the old and the new. To the student of Updike, the familiar feature of *Of the Farm* is its biographical character study. When we read the first line, "We turned off the Turnpike onto a macadam highway, then off the macadam onto a pink dirt road" (3), we know exactly where we are going, for if we have read Updike we've been there many times. We've taken the same route with several of the boys and young men of the short stories and with Peter and his father in *The Centaur*. We know exactly who will meet us at the house. We might even wonder what can possibly have been left unsaid about this particular farm and the people who live here. The ride is pleasant, however, and we soon find ourselves willing to listen to the narration which, while showing us again the fields, the house, the tractor, permits us one more visit with a woman who represents the past and will die with it. The author wants us to hear her philosophy and to look again at life before subdivision, to know once more the fierce love of the land which was a hallmark of our forbears. He wants us to listen, one more time, to a person who believed that living close to the soil meant living close to God. It will be a novel about an American mother and about a generation rapidly disappearing.

It might even be safe to assume that it is about Updike's mother. The woman who meets us at the house is one we have met several times and have come to accept as the author's mother. There are other reasons to suppose that the story of Mrs. Robinson is somewhat biographical. *Poorhouse Fair* is partly a character sketch of Updike's grandfather. *The Centaur* pays tribute in a similar way to Updike's father and is broadly autobiographical. *Of the Farm* seems to complete a trilogy by painting a portrait of the novelist's mother. Whether or not the portrait is an exact likeness is not important. The canvas is a masterpiece.

Updike does not eulogize the character of Mrs. Robinson. He creates her complete with eccentricities and virtues, with gray shadows and dashes of brilliant color. Only a "grim echo" of her youthful self, she is still vigorously unique. Witty and subtle, she can manipulate a conversation as if it were a searchlight to bluntly reveal the weaknesses of others but can turn off the switch before exposing herself. She has insight and a sense of truth about the conduct of others and a convenient blindness regarding her own motives in life. Typical of her inconsistencies and of advanced age, she has been vicious to Joey's infant son, reading motives into his innocent behavior, but visits intelligently and gently with Joey's stepson. She is cruel to her daughter-in-law but anxious not to burden her son with her illness and pending death. Complex as life itself, hers is a portrait revealing new shades of meaning each time it is examined. The integrity with which Updike has created Mrs. Robinson is one of the most commendable features of the book.

Complex and unpredictable, she is consistent in one way. She loves the land. Resisting pressures of creeping suburbanism, she has kept her farm, protective of every

fence post and crumbling brick. During a tense scene
with Joey and his wife, Mrs. Robinson explains that all
she ever wanted in life were a horse when she was a child,
and, when she became an adult, her son and her farm.
Her husband had "let" her have the son and the farm.
To these she has devoted her life. Here and there in the
Updike poetry and short stories are suggestions that
nature has some answers for seekers after Truth. His
account of Mary Robinson's fulfillment in her land is
another of these suggestions. Mrs. Robinson is not one of
Updike's searchers, but she is a woman whose life has
had purpose. The author seems to say, "Here, unattrac-
tive but real, is a woman who has found answers sufficient
for her needs. She has had little of what we commonly
consider the essentials for happiness, but, possessing and
living close to the soil, she has been fulfilled." Perhaps
she has touched God.

She says, "I believe only in what I can see or touch."
Richard, Joey's stepson, having the unclouded insight of
a child, anticipates and challenges her at the same time:
"And God," he says. Knowing that "God" does not
mean the same thing to Richard as it does to herself, she
assures him, "I see and touch God all the time. If I
couldn't see and touch Him here on the farm, if I lived
in New York City, I don't know if I'd believe or not"
(70).

The narrator explains that his mother has "religiosity
. . . unaccompanied by belief" (141), and yet she declares that God is manifest in her land. In Mrs. Robinson's opinion, living close to the soil and at a distance
from other people, being able to "touch" God in nature
is essential to man's wholeness. "I don't think God
meant people to live on *less* than eighty acres" (68), she
says. ". . . the people are growing corners so they can fit
in their little square yards better. People were meant to
be round" (69). Mrs. Robinson is "round." There are no

beginnings and no end to the nuances of her personality. She cannot be measured by a standard straightedge of character interpretation. She doesn't "believe" and yet she "touches" God. She doesn't believe but she reveals the kind of faith which needs only nature's proximity to sustain it.

Showing no evidence of belief in life for man after death, she nevertheless associates man's life with the earth's eternity. Man and the soil are closely related. "Land is just like a person, except that it never dies" (24). Knowing that her death is pending, she takes comfort from her kinship to the soil. She refuses to leave the farm for "safer" surroundings because of her wish to become one with the earth which "never dies."

If she could, she would bequeath her children her faith and her devotion to nature. She would leave to them the wisdom which crowns her age, but she knows that they will not—cannot—accept it. The fulfillment that the land has given her and her contemporaries will not be understood by her son's generation. An obvious, tangible gift from God, the land, "the earth and the fullness thereof," will be ignored. A part of America's treasured inheritance will be lost when those who understood it are gone. Joey's generation will not be able to "touch" God.

Joey, incapable of inheriting his mother's vague concept of God or her devotion to the land has, nevertheless, accepted one of her gifts, distorting it dangerously in the transfer from her philosophy to his. It is the wish for personal freedom. Mrs. Robinson has had the freedom to do what she wanted to do with her life. She is what she has willed herself to be. Freedom to her had not meant freedom from her husband or from responsibility to her son, however. It had meant freedom to live independent of dogmas and social encumbrances, freedom to give her husband and her son their freedom. To Joey freedom simply means doing what he wishes without regard for any other human being. It means freedom from the responsibility of giving himself, even to his own children. The concept of freedom which includes responsibility is another treasure which will be buried with Mrs. Robinson.

In the artistic sense, Mary Robinson and her land are Updike's symbols of the dying past. Closely identified with the farm, she and the values she represents will disappear with it. As in *The Centaur* where Caldwell and his car decay in symbolic parallel, Mary Robinson and her farm will die together. As was also true of Caldwell, the character portrait of Mrs. Robinson is complex, ambiguous. She is perplexing, but she is real, an appropriate symbol of her bewildering generation. In her story as in *The Poorhouse Fair*, another novel about the dying past, there are inefficacies of an era we should erase but also treasures of experience and belief which we should incorporate into our lives. The author helps us to distinguish between the fallacies and the treasures, but his young characters close their eyes to all.

Since Mrs. Robinson is apparently a biography, at least in part, an obvious assumption arises: Joey Robinson must be autobiographical. The fact that the author reveals convictions contrary to Joey's should discredit this assumption. As is necessary with most fiction, the novelist must creep inside the frame of the person being developed if the character is to come to life and breathe and eat and think. But he must do more than that if the portrayal is to be autobiographical. In the latter case the writer must share convictions with his double. In this novel the author shares convictions with Mrs. Robinson, not with her son. Joey has been raised on a farm which, used again and again in the author's fiction, seems to be Updike's farm. Joey's father, now deceased, seems to have been the same school teacher we met in *The Centaur*; the grandparents are also familiar. The house, its kitchen, its stairway, its bedrooms are familiar, but Joey is not. Joey fits approximately into the chronology of Updike's life, but he is not Updike.

Joey is young America—or at least part of it. He represents the self-indulgent of the new generation. In him we see their habit of abundance, lack of responsibility, preoccupation with sex. It is through Joey that Updike illustrates the young modern in an already free society who interprets all his selfish wishes as a need for freedom.

He wants freedom to possess and to discard all things at will. Though his childhood had been spent in relative poverty, indulgent parents had seen that he never lacked anything he really needed. He shows no abnormal concern about *acquiring* material things. He has them. He expects them. He accepts abundance as his birthright. With his habit of plenty is coupled an irresponsibility of ownership. He does as he pleases with what he owns, discarding at will whatever is no longer wanted. His drive is not to *get* but to *have*, to possess. Possession of more than one needs eventually demands giving or discarding. He discards.

Ownership without responsibility includes other than material things. As he has been possessed by a doting mother, he wishes to possess, to own others, not for the sake of loving but for the sake of having. There is nothing in his experience which demands giving. Discarding requires nothing and is easier than giving. It is a sign of plenty. Peggy, his bride, forgetting that Joey has possessed and discarded one wife, notices with pleasure that he acts as if he "owns" her (82). But Joey, observing that both his wife and his mother are big women, says, "It seemed a sign of great wealth that I could afford to snub them" (62).

The habit of possessing whatever one wants and discarding at will, especially when it is carried over into human relationships including that of the marriage partner, makes the second kind of freedom, freedom in sex, hardly distinguishable from the first. Joey and those of his generation he represents expect complete freedom in sex. They consider sexual attraction of greater value than all other human attributes. Joey knows that Peggy is not highly intelligent, that she is inadequate in many ways. He is even able to see her from his mother's point of view as "vulgar" (141), but these things seem not to matter, for she is "a retreating white skirt whose glimmering breadth [is] the center, the seat, of my life" (8). Love is of secondary importance if of any at all. Having discarded his first wife and children, all of whom he admits he still loves, he tells his mother that he has what he wants. "I'm all right, money, sex, everything" (36). His needs and his wealth are summed up in two specific categories, money and sex, with the latter the more important.

Money can be had from the land, but Joey seems to be in no hurry to sell the farm. As he likes possessing women, he likes possessing the land. Now and then he nostalgically considers its natural beauties or its real potential, but his wife is right; in the final analysis, he likes the farm in the same way he likes her as "something big you can show off" (122).

Owning land is related to, interwoven with the possessive aspects of sex. "My wife is wide . . . and, surveyed from above, gives an impression of terrain, of wealth whose ownership imposes upon my own body a sweet strain of extension" (46). Possession, becoming one with sex, however illogically, evolves next into freedom. "With Peggy I skim, I glide, I am free, and this freedom, once tasted, lightly, illicitly, became as indispensable as oxygen to me" (47). One cannot live without oxygen; if oxygen and freedom in sex are one and the same, love of wife and children can mean little. To Joey they mean only an occasional twinge of guilt. Nothing other than sex and "freedom" is important.

Joey is not the only character in the story who has interpreted his selfishness as a wish for freedom. Peggy has gained her freedom from her first husband that she, in turn, may be free in sexual encounters. Mrs. Robinson had seen her selfish wish to live on the farm as a kind of freedom she and everyone else deserves and wants. Her husband had not shared her devotion to rural life. By including others in her wishes, she rationalizes her selfishness into social concern. She dreams of the farm as "a people sanctuary" (71) where city dwellers can get away from their confinement of crowds. That others might not want her kind of freedom does not occur to her.

The Robinsons' selfish concepts of personal freedom are symptom of errors of the past and cause of mistakes of the present. Joey and his wife have forgotten that personal freedom always demands responsibility. Mrs. Robinson is unaware that her freedom has deprived others of freedom as they saw it. No one person in a free society can be entirely free if others are to have a like measure of freedom.

Updike sympathizes with the Robinsons, but he does not agree with them on this point. He has created them in the likeness of people as they are, not as they should be. Their concept of personal freedom is the epitome of misinterpretation in the generation dying and the one just launching its career. The author's attitude is expressed in a quotation from Sartre which prefaces the novel:

Consequently, when, in all honesty, I've recognized that man is a being in whom existence precedes essence, that he is a free being who, in various circumstances, can want only his freedom, I have at the same time recognized that I can want only the freedom of others.

Mrs. Robinson, allowing herself to believe that she has wanted the freedom of others, comes closer to embracing the existentialist's philosophy than does her son, Joey, but both deceive themselves. Mrs. Robinson can see freedom for others only through her own definition of freedom. Joey is "a free being who . . . can want only his freedom . . ." but certainly demonstrates that he is not in the least concerned about wanting "the freedom of others."

The third major emphasis in *Of the Farm* is the theme of change. The motif is present in the author's poetry and continues forcefully here. Change is inevitable: ". . . the clothes which, setting out, we packed / With love no longer fit when we arrive." Joey is not what his mother willed him to be, cannot live entirely by her example. She has not lived in the example of her parents. As useful as the mores of the past generation might have been to its children, they will not serve those of the present. Some things will carry over—such as the love for freedom—but they will be altered as all things are altered with the passing of time.

The Joey Robinson who looks out of the portraits hung on the living room wall in the farm home is not the same as the one who brings his second wife to the scene of his childhood. He has departed from his past physically and emotionally. Except for his tendency toward self-indulgence, he seems never to have been the coddled only child for whose attention his mother now struggles with his wife. He is a stranger, a guide leading tourists through the museum of his past. He has severed himself from his childhood and from his early maturity, from his children and their mother. His first wife is a "flat pose" in a frame on the wall. His children appear only as distortions in his dreams. Family relationships, tradition, even faith have changed.

Symbolically, the family Bible rests "neglected, heavy as a casket" (38) in a lowly position near the floor in a room rarely used. Caskets hold dead things, in this case the once-important genealogy and the revered Christian customs of the family. At one point in the story, speaking of his new family, Joey says, "Their un-thinking non-Christianity sometimes worried me, and I blamed myself for having never gathered the nerve to teach Richard a good-night prayer, as I had done with my own children" (129). But this is the only indication that Joey at any time had been concerned about abandoning Christian practices or even had considered himself a Christian. Christianity has been casually set aside with the family Bible. Things have changed.

Joey has changed. Christian rituals have been abandoned. The farm is fading and dying. The "vultures" of real estate watch nearby for the right moment to dismember the dead thing which was a way of life to Mary Robinson and her generation but is an odious encumbrance to her son. His contemporaries will replant it with small square houses and cement. There will be a new way of life to replace the old.

One aspect of the new life, divorce, instituted in the name of compassion and reason and once the exception, has become to the Joeys a common stage of development in man's progress toward freedom. Updike's *Of the Farm* and numerous short stories appearing in publication sequence with it deal more and more frequently with divorce. Divorce—separation from one's personal commitments—is one with society's separation from the God of its past. When departure from sacred commitments is complete and God is forgotten, of what significance are pledges to a mere spouse or to one's children?

Children, the issue of "freedom" without responsibility, are lonely and tragic, forced into early independence and self-sufficiency. The two children most vividly portrayed in *Of the Farm* are Charlie and Richard, sons of the newlyweds by former spouses. Richard, intelligent and precocious from the habit of playing the adult protector of his mother, is hurrying through childhood toward the safer stage already reached by his stepfather where responsibility does not necessarily result from one's willful behavior. While the child strains toward adulthood, the stepfather, Joey, envies the boy's relationship to Peggy, wanting "to be his size and to go to her" (118). He wants to be protected and mothered as the child should be.

As for Charlie, Joey's natural son, he appears only in a dream as an homunculus, a wretched, stunted creature, but Joey permits Charlie's problems to concern him nowhere except in his dreams. Freedom to satisfy one's thirst is much more important than the pain of an abandoned and desolate child. The bad dreams, the lonely children will vanish. Their problems will be drowned in the cool content of satisfied thirsts which his new wife makes possible. Divorce amends codes of responsibility, accommodates life's "unavoidable" changes. Richard and Charlie are the tragic result of change rationalized as the inevitable.

Change is not only a *theme* in *Of the Farm*; it is a *fact*. This novel marks changes in the author's direction. It is the beginning of new trends in character portrayal, new topics, new emphases. It even heralds a new public image of Updike himself.

When, in November 1966, *Life* headed an Updike feature by Jane Howard, "Can a Nice Novelist Finish First?" the reader knew by the title's implication that Updike's novels were not competing with the current literary trend in sensationalism. *Rabbit, Run* created a mild sensation, but *Of the Farm* is, by comparison, a pale pastoral, a reader's sedative. Though dealing with the subjects of divorce and sex, it is not dirty and certainly not sensational. As a matter of fact, every earthy or sensual paragraph is budding with delicate wild flowers of good taste. The deft handling of topics often exploited by contemporary novelists for their sale value distinguishes the work, elevates it far above the level of marketable sensation. This novel evinces no need on the part of the author to compete with bookstand bawdry. But it paves the way for new things and forms a transition between the earlier novels and *Couples*, the one to follow. It announces subtly that sex is a topic in itself, one which consumes the attention of the Joeys. It prepares us to meet people to whom Joey is a novice indeed. The book suggests that Updike, if he wishes, can compete with cheap sensationalism without becoming a cheap sensationalist.

Of the Farm introduces a change in the makeup of Updike characters. Harry Angstrom of *Rabbit, Run* is a nearly hopeless egoist, but even he evinces a spark of purpose in life. He believes that waiting for him somewhere is something good to give his life direction. When he walks away from his child's grave and out of the story, the reader, approving of very little he has done, nevertheless sympathizes with the pathetic young man and hopes with him for the eventual discovery of the "something" that wants him to find it. According to critic David Galloway, Rabbit is among the "absurd saints" [1] typical of Updike's first novels. In his misguided way, he strikes out at the fumbling society which has created him. Something like this is true of the three principals of the three early novels. *Of the Farm*, the fourth, features no saints unless Mrs. Robinson is one of them. Joey Robinson reflects the social chaos in which he lives, but he neither seeks nor is aware that he needs a way out. Rabbit knows that he is in trouble. Joey, a character with more intellectual potential than a dozen Harry Angstroms, is content with existing as close as possible to the skirt which is the "center, the seat" of his life. He is what we see and no more. There is no hope for improvement. He is a new kind of leading character in Updike fiction.

The changes in topics and types of characters herald

other innovations as well. *Of the Farm*, completing a trilogy which pays tribute to members of his immediate family, may well be the last of the semibiographical works of Updike. The family has been covered. The author admits in the foreword to *Olinger Stories* to having written so many pieces in the "Olinger" setting and about a character who, though wearing different names, "is at bottom the same boy" (v), that an autobiography is "impossible" (vi). The young "John" to be examined in the chapter on short stories, does not appear in this novel and probably will not in succeeding ones. "John" and the "absurd saints" support the author's early theme of goodness in all men. If we have seen the last of "John" and "Olinger," we may have heard the last of the themes to which they are related. But there will be other character portrayals like that of Joey. There will be people whose interests are limited to sex and self. There will be new, despairing philosophies to examine if *Of the Farm* is a prediction.

Another distinguishing feature of Updike's early novels which is absent from this transition work is an air of optimism. If hope exists in this story at all, it is in the child, Richard. Skillfully portrayed, he comes to life before us. He has a glow of happy potential. Among the four people who spend a weekend on the farm, he is the most mature and reasonable. He smooths the creased fabrics of jealousy with forthrightness and simplicity. He is selfless enough to be concerned about others, even a quarrelsome old woman who uses him as hostage when her would-be attackers come closest to threats of abandonment. He actually finds something to like about the woman whose son merely tolerates her. Unlike his stepfather (whom the boy also likes), Richard has not yet limited his interests to physical fulfillment. He is curious about everything new, eager to learn, unspoiled by parental indulgence. Because he is promising, he becomes a tragic figure when we realize that there is almost no chance for him to develop into anything but another Joey. There is nothing to suggest that he will take any route other than that of his parents, natural or substitute. He will learn from example and influence. Bred in an environment of selfishness and willful disregard for others, he will probably learn selfishness and willful disregard for others, conveniently interpreting his conduct, as his teachers do, as personal freedom. The optimism which gave the early Updike novels a buoyant quality is not present here.

The failure to discover anything hopeful in *Of the Farm*, particularly in the character of Joey Robinson, should not be construed as ignorance of the poetic nature the author gives his leading character. Joey, who narrates the story, *thinks* in eloquent rhetoric. Herein lies a major inconsistency in the artistic structure of the book. It is difficult to accept the shallow, egoistic Joey as one and the same with the man who tells the story. He tells us that "Diagonal shafts of sun and shadow and vapor streamed earthward from glowing citadels of cumulus spaced as if strategically across the illusory continent above . . ." (72). It seems to be someone other than Joey who, when taking a drink of water from a tin measuring cup tells the reader, "Its calibrated sides became at my lips the walls of a cave where my breath rustled and cold well water swayed" (66). Only in discourse with the reader does Joey communicate in this fashion. In dialogue with other characters, his speech is mundane.

> I asked my mother, "What whispering?"
> "You were whispering. I heard Richard whispering."
> "He was asking me why it was so quiet," Peggy said.
> "Well why *is* it?"
> "You know damn well why," Peggy said. "You're throwing a sulk and worrying your son."

"My son? My son worries me. He says I killed his father."
I said, "I never said that. . . ."

"I'm tired," she said, "of being hated. I've lost everything but this child's respect and I don't want him whispering."

"Nobody hates you."

"Well I'm tired," Peggy said, "of this. . . . I'm not going to keep Richard exposed to so much neuroticism . . . we'll both feel better if I go."

"It's night," I said. (117–18)

Joey, in speech is uninspired. "I never said that." "Nobody hates you." "It's night." His responses in the book's heat of conflict are in keeping with his "I could care less" conduct but not with his style of reporting.

Joey as a man with poetic insight and a genius for reporting the sights and sounds of a beautiful world while destroying his own children and permitting his own nothingness of existence is either too tragic to bear or too inconsistent to believe. The reader is forced to attempt a compromise: The book is a stage on which Joey acts the role, speaks the lines. By remote control, a second speaker, sophisticated and eloquently articulate, dubs in the narration for the inadequate performer. There is no mistaking one for the other. Updike is the narrator. Joey Robinson is the actor.

The author's purpose in this matter is not clear. Had Updike told Joey's story from an omniscient point of view, there would have been no problem. In the first person, he develops inconsistencies which the reader finds difficult to compromise. Joey has artistic powers not in keeping with his limited insights and his singular physical responses. Capable of sensing delicate relationships between a butterfly and a field shorn of its wildflowers, he is nevertheless insensitive to human emotions and need. The reader waits patiently for Joey to make a profound discovery about his own failures as a man but none is forthcoming. There are two Joeys who have never met.

In one scene toward the end of the novel, the poet in the guise of Joey Robinson tells Richard a story. The reader observes, "Here comes Updike to make a major point." That is exactly what happens, for Joey, a man who exists to satisfy his own lust and for little else would not have cared, and the point needs to be made. Had Joey *read* a story to Richard, we could believe, but the Joey Robinson who waits for his mother to die so that his weekends will be less complicated is not the one who creates for Richard the story of the frog in the rain. Updike tells the story.

While being pelted with rain, symbolically life's problems, Frog turns to the depths of his inner being to search for identity and becomes smaller and smaller until he disappears. Updike's early theme of man's endless search suddenly flashes in neon brillance. Man searches his mind and soul for self-significance, for the treasure of Truth, only to become less and less significant in the vastness of his own perplexing makeup and in the infinite scope of the universe. This cannot be Joey's story, for *he* is the soul and center of his universe; he searches for nothing in himself and little elsewhere. He is not Frog.

At the point of Frog's disappearance, Richard asks, "Is that the end? . . . He died?" The narrator replies, "Who said he died? He just became so small he couldn't find himself. He was hibernating." The reader would like to believe that Joey has recognized that he has become so "small" he can't find himself and that after taking time out to think things over he might live again, refreshed and wise, but it is Updike, not Joey who speaks. The author in parable superb goes on.

"You really think death is disappearing?"
"I don't know."
"Good. I don't either. Anyway, after a while in the spring, the frog woke up, looked around in the darkness, ran up

through the rooms, up the circular stairs, to his eyes, threw open the lids, and looked out. And the sky was blue. End of story." (131)

Frog doesn't die. Disappearing is not death. Man doesn't find answers in self-searching, in self-centeredness. When he looks *out* and around him, there is no further need for search. Life is a blue sky and offers all the purpose one needs. The concept that looking outward and beyond oneself gives life its meaning is not a Joey Robinson discovery. He searches for nothing but sexual fulfillment. He spends no time on introspection. Neither does he look out at the world or he would see his mother, his children, perhaps even his children's mother. We can accept "The Frog in the Rain" only as an Updike story, not a Joey Robinson one.

The allusion in the story to another Updike concept, man's significant minuteness, is not a Joey Robinson idea, either. It is a restatement of the theme of Updike's poem "Mobile of Birds." Man, "so small inside," so frog-like, in a vast, dark dungeon of endless incomprehensibility is like the bird, alone but essential to the balance of all things else in the cavern of space and time. Joey Robinson never questions his significance, and concern for things outside himself is completely foreign to his character. We can conclude only that Updike tells the story "The Frog in the Rain" as a reassuring contrast to the meaninglessness of Joey's life and as a conclusion to an account of hopeless selfishness with "and yet—and yet. . . ."

Frog has been present with other identities in other Updike works; the reader is relieved to meet him again, for he is a promise that with the introduction of new characters and themes, the author's purposes have not entirely changed. Whether his characters depict it or not, perhaps John Updike, like Frog, will continue to provide a "yea-saying to the goodness and joy of life."

7

Couples

Of the Farm promises, through its transitory nature, to lead to something new. It does. *Couples* is new. John Updike's fifth novel is an adventure, a frontier, new ground for the author and his readers. The complaint of some of the critics and other literary scholars that it does not fulfill the promise of the Updike genius, that it does not satisfy the waiting public, comes because of lack of understanding of that genius and of that waiting public. The criticism is a result of a preconceived idea of what the author's fifth novel *should* be. It comes from an academic notion—but not a definition—of what a great novel is. Conventionality is not prepared for the frontier which *Couples* reaches and explores.

In the minds of some, even frontiers are limited to preconceived criteria. Updike, who frequently makes reference to Paul Tillich, might well have gained courage from that theological frontiersman to explore a borderland quite foreign to his earlier works. Tillich describes the man who fears the different as a "Philistine."

Regardless of what social class he appears in, he can be exactly characterized as someone who—because of his anxiety at reaching his own frontier and seeing himself in the mirror of the different—can never risk rising above the habitual, the recognized, the established.[1]

John Updike is no "Philistine." Not afraid to be different, he has risen above the "habitual, the recognized, the established." He leaves the homeland of his introspective idealism and suffering heroes and crosses into an era where the view is outward, where the principal characters are unrelated to the author's experience and only in minor ways to his personal philosophy. The frontier is his own—not that mapped for him by his critics. Because it is not what was expected, many do not understand it and become, themselves, Tillich "Philistines" who are unable to cross with him. Because they do not know where he is going, they refuse to agree to the value of the exploration.

As was suggested in the discussion of the earlier novel, *Of the Farm*, that he might, Updike, in *Couples*, competes with cheap sensationalism without becoming a cheap sensationalist. It should be no surprise to those who have followed his work diligently that he has written a book which satisfies the seeker of thrills as well as the searcher after Truth. From his earliest writing he has been predicting this book. In the autobiography of his childhood, "The Dogwood Tree: A Boyhood," [2] he speaks of "Three Great Secret Things: (1) Sex (2) Religion (3) Art." All three are present in all his fiction, but in *Couples* they change positions of significance. No one is independent of the other; all are interwoven into one fabric, but one fiber, sex, is dominant. The three, phrased in Biblical cadence, bring to mind the Corinthian aphorism which has inspired the founding of everything from great, permanent churches to more temporary Hippy movements. "Faith, hope, love, these three, and the greatest of these is love." It is not difficult to imagine a parallel between Updike's "three great secret things" and the "ambiloquent" Christian axiom. In such analogy, "love" becomes "sex" as it is often interpreted in American society. The new phrasing of the parallel is anticipated before it can be written: "the greatest of these is sex." That sex preoccupies the lives of the principals in *Couples* can hardly be disputed. If the story is an account of Americans as they really live, the book and its subject need no justification. Updike's new emphasis should be no surprise. That the public will read a new book with sex as its subject should also be no surprise. That such a book can be written as though it were a frontier, an unexplored land of meaning and inspiration, a topic from which to create new art *is* surprising, perhaps remarkable. John Updike is a remarkable artist.

Regardless of subject, the primary objective of the artist is to create. The literary artist may strive to create things beautiful, to reproduce precisely what he sees, to invent reality from his imagination, to stir emotions, to phrase a message or a philosophy, or sometimes, like many a modern painter, to create that which will startle. He may attempt all, but to accomplish all in one work is to reach an artistic ultimate. In *Couples* John Updike approaches that ultimate.

As always, he creates things beautiful. There is one point on which his critics all agree. His style is superb. His work is worth reading if for no reason other than to enjoy the piquant phrase, the lyric vision, the fluent rhetoric. The style of *Couples* is not new, for it is familiarly Updike's, yet it is ever new because it is uniquely his. Refined from volume to volume, the Updike style approaches disciplined perfection in *Couples*.

One technique which emerges again and again with ever-startling effect is the prophecy by reflective imagery. A simple account of a scene or an event is made, and suddenly a foreknowing of things to come is certain and clear. Experiencing ill fortune and personal weakness, a builder who has taught an ambitious young man the skills of his trade visits the home of the apprentice where the kitchen "seemed the snug galley of a ship on its way to warmer waters" (452). The scene flashes a message to the reader as if it were an NBC bulletin. The unstable benefactor and teacher will be usurped by his apprentice.

An emotion, compressed into a brief and effortless sentence or phrase, announces with certainty that a man will die. "John lit a cigarette and suffered a fit of dry coughing. . . . An elemental vocabulary among all men. The cough, the laugh, the sob, the scream, the fart, the sigh. Amen" (190).

Two women, one of them young and beautiful and new in town, the other the builder's dependable wife, are visiting casually. The newcomer wants the other's husband to remodel her house. In only a sentence we learn that the younger woman will create discord in the marriage of the older one. It is a subtle but certain prophecy. Angela, the exemplary wife "went on hesitatingly, as if her choice of words were distracted by a flowering of things unseen" (67). The flowering occurs, the quick, bold blooming of a weed which suffocates the cultivated but undernourished plant of Angela's marriage.

There is little suspense created by these foreshadowings, for they tell us all, but their delicate precision, their own refreshing small surprises of form, banish any need for tricks of plotting to keep the reader's attention.

The visible commentary is another technique which distinguishes Updike's style. He wastes no time digressing with wordy opinions or lectures. The young woman who destroys a marriage for the sake of her sexual appetites also agrees to destroy a life—that of her own baby —by abortion. The author reveals his attitude in the matter through a small, sad scene. A door opens onto a dark alley in the impersonal center of the city. A Negress in a green uniform supports the young woman who has permitted destruction of her unborn child. The woman is helped into the waiting car by a male companion. "The Negress in silence closed the metal door upon herself. She had not stepped into the alley." She doesn't just close the door; she stands aloof from the scene in the alley, and from her superior, uncontaminated position, puts a firm barrier between herself and the event.

After departure of the automobile, "a condom and candy wrapper lay paired in the exposed gutter" (378). Symbols of satisfied appetites and open sewers combine. The *visible commentary*, an Updike technique, is complete.

From such skill come sunny scenes as well as sordid. The reader who enjoys children will return to Updike's depictions of them for more than one observation. They seem to promise, like the fact of a child's existence, that all is not without hope, no matter how low the adults have fallen. The novelist presents children as they really are: "Nancy hung back near the birdbath and, thumb in mouth, fanned her fingers as if to hide her face" (63). He takes care to dress them in colors and costumes to distinguish them from or to blend them with their surroundings as circumstances suggest. The reader experiences the tenderness of the morning when Nancy, "huddled in her pink nightie on the brown living-room sofa in the shadowless early morning light" (75) shares the scene with her gentle mother who wears a blue robe and her confident sister who, in a yellow Easter coat, goes off to school in a yellow bus. There is no burden of cute detail; yet nothing needed for sensitive, artistic balance is missing.

Complements to character such as color and costume are extended to cars and houses for the adults. Reminiscent of Caldwell's symbolic double in his hearselike secondhand Buick in *The Centaur*, automobiles are paired painstakingly with their owners. One of the wealthy couples who are anxious to live life fully by doing things for themselves and being unpretentious and casual, drive a secondhand maroon Mercury. Foxy, a woman of many temperaments, drives a station wagon of "hymnal blue" when, in the eyes of her lover, she is a glad song for a Sunday morning. When she is her "other self," demanding and willful, quick and determined, she is seen in her husband's M.G., slamming doors with finality, departing from church in a burst of conscienceless self-assurance. Her lover drives a pickup. Capable of hard work, he is earthy and unrefined, simple and unrestrained. Sweating in the middle of a hard day's work, he takes a woman as he would a drink of water, drinking deep of cool content. During the one year covered by the story, four wives other than his own cooperate in satisfying his thirst. To each tryst he drives the belching pickup truck which, month after month, wears a "wash me" sign scribbled on its tail gate—not on its door but its *tail gate*. It is no accident that the car reflects its owner boldly as well as in subtle details.

Houses, too, are built by the author to complement the people he creates to live in them. The careless but beautiful Foxy who has "a constant blush like windburn or fever" (13) and wears billowing maternity clothes and loose, flowing hair styles, who takes her freedom at all costs, willfully wooing the builder while she is carrying her husband's child, lives in an expensive but carelessly built and excitingly unusual seaside house from which the view is ever-changing over the marshes ever green. The builder, "in love with right-angled things" (5), provides for his faithful wife and adored children a square and solid and conventional house some miles from the destructive sea winds and unstable sands. It is not the house his wife wants, but it is the one he wants for her, and it reflects his attitudes about her and about the kind of man he would be if his will were as strong as his impulses. For numerous characters there are houses distinctly different and appropriate, their descriptions as complete as a researched report on New England architecture. And yet the people who live in them are anything but researched and documented. They are "live." The people of Tarbox live and breathe in houses designed for them by a sensitive craftsman who *knows* his characters.

Colors, cars, houses, symbols and signs are Updike tradition but are never used in excess. A symbol which is strained and contrived serves only to detract from the work of which it is a part, but when used with restraint and skill can immeasurably enhance the total effect of a writer's work. The carefully devised man-beast which doubled for Caldwell in *The Centaur* did, for some readers, interfere with the novelist's art rather than enrich it. In *Couples* this problem does not exist. The symbolism employed is quiet in tone, hardly noticeable on the canvas until the reader takes a second look. The names of principal characters, innocently ordinary at first glance, become ironically allegorical as their significance is made obvious. Angela is the gracious mother and faithful wife whose name mocks her after, in an effort to save herself from hopeless neuroticism, she finally imitates the behavior of women who have been her husband's mistresses. Foxy, a flaxen-haired beauty with an apparently innocent blush is as treacherous as the proverbial little beast whose name she bears. Freddy Thorne is barely tolerated because of his crude mannerisms and sharp tongue even though the others in the crowd are hardly sweet-smelling roses. Piet Hanema, the only one who goes to church and the one with whom any one of the women would break a wedding vow, does not accidentally have a name which looks like "piety" with a capital "P." After the acerbity of the story has worn off, the reader can imagine the fun the author must have had as he created Piet, the man who drives from the house of his mistress to the church of his faith in his truck with the "wash me" tail gate.

Even the name of the town which is the setting for the story has a metaphorical ring. "Tarbox" phonetically resembles the "ticky-tacky" boxes or houses of middle-classdom as described in a song popular within the last decade. The subject of the futility of life in affluent middle-class suburbs could hardly find a more appropriate setting than "Tarbox," the town whose name suggests the texture of heated earthiness. "Smithville" or "Pleasant Grove" might have been more typical, but "Tarbox" has the right smell.

Other symbols more familiar to Updike readers are also present in *Couples*. The inaccessible stars appear as they did in *The Centaur*, with significance as obvious as their presence but as difficult to comprehend. Angela, the good wife, knows their names and constellations. Piet, the wayward husband, at one point looks to them in a moment of trouble and decides that there is little he can do about his mistakes since "the future is in the sky after all. Everything already exists" (273). Freddy, the dentist and would-be friend says, "there is nothing to steer by but sex and stoicism and the stars" (372). Updike uses the stars again as unexplained assurance of permanence.

Closer to earth, neon lights, invariably present in Updike's lonely city scenes, burn through a mist over a "somber little pavilion" (373) on Boston Common while Piet waits, alone and afraid, hoping for a baby to die and a mistress to live. In Updike fiction, times of fear, loneliness, and death are accompanied frequently by blatant neon lights which burn dispassionately in the impersonal cities.

Symbols representing the church are present in all the novels and appear in *Couples* as ironic emphasis of nonbelief or of moral degradation. Harry Angstrom in *Rabbit, Run* seeks comfort in a scene at the church across the street from the room he and his mistress share on a Sunday morning. Piet in *Couples* makes love to another man's wife "on the Sunday morning, beneath the hanging clangor of bells" (435). Faintly aware that his way of life and that of his crowd is somewhat less than exemplary, Piet has visions of the church but is so nearly immune to their message that his mind registers only a

"stately hollow blur" (244). The author's church symbols clearly suggest to many of the characters beauty
empty of meaning and to the reader the bitter irony of a
message unheeded.

Symbolic as are their names and setting, Updike's
characters are people—some shallow, all complex, all real.
They are not people with whom the reader can necessarily identify, but neither are many of our real neighbors. They are not people who live in a town that *could*
exist. They are people who live in a town and a social
circle which *do* exist in the mind of their creator. Like
them or not, we have to admit that such people are a
part of flesh and blood society. The artist may paint an
impressionistic canvas or a realistic one. The novelist
may write a book of fantasy or a story of life as it is.
Couples relates life as it is. Updike does not say, "This
is the way we all live" but "This is the way these people
in Tarbox live. If they look and act like people in Pleasant Grove and Smithville and Anywhere, U.S.A., do not
be surprised, for the resemblance is intended." They
aren't *exactly* like the people of Pleasant Grove, however. They are Piet and Angela and Foxy and Freddy of
Tarbox, and they are real.

Piet and Foxy and Angela and Freddy are singularly
Updike's creations even though they resemble possibly
thousands of Americans. They have the unique qualities
of the art of which they are a part. Each is an individual
as distinctly as is each of our neighbors. No matter how
typical a neighbor might be, in reality he *is* Albia Snow-
shaker, not John Typical Doe, no matter how much they
resemble one another. Each character created by Updike
is distinctly *that* character and no other.

Some critics of Updike, including many not in print,
insist that the novelist has written *Couples* for the express purpose of its shock value. There is an indisputable
tendency among contemporary writers, painters, and

sculptors of uncertain significance to demand attention by shocking. Many artists seem to say, instead of "See what I have created," "Look! Ha! Shocked you, didn't I? You *will* notice me." Others must say to themselves, "My work is meaningless and therefore more mysterious than another. Because you find no meaning in it and no feeling for it, you will wonder what obscure greatness you have witnessed and will remember me." Such "art" serves no function other than to get attention, for attention is all the "artist" seeks. Art of this level and of these points of view is in keeping with the desperate "Notice-me-I-am-an-individual-not-just-a-bubble-in-the-detergent-of-humanity" attitude prevalent in the present decade. The need to be noticed is observed in clothing, hair styles, and conduct as well as in art forms and is more prevalent than the need to create. It is, of course, present in many contemporary novels, some of which have nothing to say and no purpose other than to get attention for their authors.

Unquestionably, the quality of shock is also a part of some of the finest of modern art which *does* have something to say. No artist in America needs less than Updike to write a shocking novel for the purpose of gaining attention. Updike has the priceless distinction of having been noticed without having resorted to the "Sex for Sale" sign which reflects alternately red and silver in the plate-glass window of the bank across the street. *Couples*, in keeping with the trend in art and social behavior, does use the shock technique, but unlike works of lesser significance, uses it for something more than the sake of the jolt.

The book is a modern art form of many dimensions. Updike's new frontier allows for new dimensions. Sex as subdued in the cool pastels of *Of the Farm* has been replaced by scenes of sex acts complete with camouflaged heating units uncontrolled by electric thermostat. In keeping with the technique of the canvas depicting in oils a woman's breasts which sprout actual plastic baby bottle nipples from Walgreen's,[3] *Couples* incorporates multidimensional media. The first effect of the painting of the breasts with mass-produced mechanical nipples is shock—perhaps even disgust, but a moment's reflection is *demanded* of the viewer, and the message makes its initial impression. In modern society the mass-produced, look-alike, look-ugly, highly functional gadget replaces the female breast as principal source of succor and comfort for the human infant. The painting has demanded attention and, that gained, pours forth possibilities for endless speculation. Like such a painting, the multidimensional novel shocks and then carries the reader on to an infinity of new ideas, involving the reader to a degree no other Updike novel has. Once the shock has served its purpose of demanding the reader's attention, the messages clatter in ticker-tape time to his fully primed intellect.

Unlike many works in oil and steel and tin cans, *Couples* has been constructed painstakingly. Even with new media, the artist still uses a carefully controlled brush of finest sable. He does not throw the paint at the canvas and let it drip to see what bizarre effect will create itself. Neither does he use plastic nipples glued to canvas. A medley of breasts in *Couples* is created by the skilled strokes of an artist who prefers realism to impression but panorama to narrow focus. The multidimensional work is produced by media in complete harmony, the total effect becoming one of reality reflected, emotions stirred, philosophies phrased. It is a story involving sex, religion, and art. It is art in *fact* and sex and religion in theme. It is a shocking, modern story about life in shocking modern times.

The second of life's "great secret things" is religion. Art is the medium. Religion emerges as a theme. No Updike novel ignores the topic, and *Couples* gains dignity because of it. The motifs which fall under the general heading of religion are not as new as the author's approach to them. That man is a lonely, confused, complex creature, that he intuitively searches for something, that he needs a religion in harmony with modernity are familiar topics to Updike readers. A theme which is not new but which receives greater emphasis than in earlier books is fear of death, and a new one, the nature of sin, its contagion and certainty of punishment, emerges with forceful impact.

One of the leading figures in *Couples* has much in common with Harry Angstrom of *Rabbit, Run,* Peter and George Caldwell of *The Centaur,* and "John" of the short stories. He is Piet Hanema, alien "member" of the social circle of twenty elite Tarbox citizens. He is the outsider, the "loner" who does not quite fit. Like the principals of earlier stories, he cannot find his niche in the framework of Tarbox social structure. He is tolerated only by virtue of his marriage to Angela Hamilton, a highly qualified candidate who gives the group what little dignity it claims. They cannot do without her; they are forced to accept her husband.

Piet, the son of humble, self-effacing Dutch immigrants, believes in God, His Church, hard work, and love. He respects his wife. He adores his children. Until his marriage to Angela who had always known the comforts of wealth and prominence, he had known only a simple life of work and humility and love. The accidents of a wartime friendship and the highway deaths of his parents have separated him from his past and catapulted him into a marriage and a social class where he is uncomfortable. The circle accepts him as an uninvited relative is accepted, dutifully but not wholeheartedly. Because he is masculine and lovable, unsophisticated and impulsive, the women woo him privately while the suspicious and jealous men tolerate him. Except when he is in bed with one of the wives, Piet is alone.

Having tried to bury his conscience in an effort to live his new role, Piet has nothing to guide him but his impulses. He wonders what bars him "from the ranks of those many blessed who [believe] nothing" (20), and wants to be one of them, but he cannot entirely disbelieve. He continues to go to church, clinging to something of his past from which he finds it difficult to separate himself but forgetting the part of it which would be a solace in his loneliness.

His conscience refuses to be buried, however, emerging for brief moments in the ghosts of his dead parents, in symbols of the church, or in bad dreams. His is an uncomfortable loneliness, not a serene solitude. At one time he dreams that he is an old minister making calls and that he stands on the median strip of a superhighway looking into the valley where he must go to serve his congregation. He finally continues across the highway and is arrested before his calls can be made. His lovable nature could have led him, perhaps, to a role in service of humanity, or at least to one of acceptance and love among people he could understand, but something, perhaps the tide of circumstance which he has made no effort to control, has prevented his taking such a road. The potential of his early character no longer exists. Without God he is alone. Now his calls of love are made in the framework of his social circle —to the beds of his friends' wives.

Confusion is a greater problem in *Couples* than is loneliness. Trying to live in the present, Piet is constantly distracted by the past and its influences. He is pictured as a man "growing old without wisdom, alert and strained" (69). Having in his youth depended on his parents and an infallible God, he now must cope with people who seem comfortable without God. He is forced to compensate, to combine his restless, unthinking faith with their comfortable, unthinking *lack* of faith. The result is total perplexity. Straining to be one of the group without joining them in disbelief, he stumbles again and again. He knows something about love. He does not know how to separate *agape* from passion nor passion from its consequences.

Complete confusion is the result. Updike's familiar topic of man's perpetual dilemma, his emotional and mental perplexity, emerges in bold relief. Piet tries to take what he wants without knowing what he wants. He applauds something precious in one act and condemns it in the next. He wants to continue in the role of the good husband and father, but he likes adultery for the sake of adultery. He wants the reassurances enjoyed by the religious, but at the same time would abandon the moral codes associated with religious belief. He goes to church but gives in to his sexual appetites without discrimination or self-discipline. He loves his daughters and would like a son, but he insists on destruction of his unborn child his mistress is carrying.

As if these of Piet's inconsistencies were not enough to illustrate the point, the novelist tells of the gentle way he handles birds with broken wings or tenderly nurses small dying creatures to life. In one scene in his house of conformity and love, Piet, in a telephone conversation with his mistress, declares with relentless finality that the child in her womb may not live. He then hangs up the telephone and receives his little daughter who comes confidently to him with a frozen bird cupped in her hands. He will do what he can to keep the bird alive. With terrible irony the author concludes the illustration of Piet's and man's tragic confusion.

As Piet is confused, so is he complex. His craft, carpentry, is placed by the author in the realm of sacred things when he speaks of the "holy odor of shavings"

(197). Piet builds solidly and well, even if without fair financial return. He likes creating things from his own design and with his own hands, a good house or a sensible cage for a hamster. His work is disciplined and chaste. He loves the natural beauties of the earth and likes to see his houses blend with their settings, but watching the earth torn by a bulldozer is painful to him. A child's tears move him, but his wife's mental anguish does not. His temperament at times approaches that of a poet. In a game of "impressions" at one of the weekend parties, he likens Foxy to a flower. "I think you're a yellow carnation they made drink purple ink, so you're this incredible black, and people keep touching you, thinking you must be artificial, and are amazed that you're an actual flower" (183). Occasionally his poetic temperament ceases to be his own and becomes, as did Joey's in *Of the Farm*, that of Updike. Much of the time, however, it is believably Piet's. A carpenter and a poet, Piet is also a man affectionate yet cruel, disciplined yet impulsive, artistic but crude, solid in one way while staggeringly weak in another. He is one of Updike's prime examples of the complexity of human character.

Foxy Whitman, his mistress and another complexity, is a person to be both pitied and admired. A girl who has devoted herself to her husband and his career, waiting and working the long years while he prepared for a profession, she has postponed motherhood and homemaking, suppressing in herself the warmth that she has always had for things small and helpless. She has wanted to give her husband, Ken, a baby and to "share God" (102) with him. She has had an apparently conventional point of view about her role in life. Now, finally, she has the home and is carrying Ken's baby. He is an assistant professor in biochemistry in a promising university. "Their reasons for happiness [are] as sweeping as the view from their new house" (43), but Foxy is not content. She willfully plans an affair with Piet, the gentle Dutchman who comes each day to remodel and rearrange and strengthen the house with the view of the sea. He is anything but resistant. The two of them knowingly complicate their lives and commit what, even in their own eyes, is sin. For it is these two who profess a respect for the church and a belief in God. It is these two in the crowd who not only verbalize a faith but seem to feel God in all things. Foxy, at a party where guests play "wonderful" by naming the most marvelous thing which comes to mind, says "The Eucharist" (240).

Reasons for Foxy's behavior can be found in her husband's chemical, impassive manner, but they do not make a good argument. He is not capable of her warmth, but he is handsome, steady, and dependable. In his way, he loves her. He is proud of her. He buys her an expensive house and does not hesitate to spend thousands more to permit her every whim in its restoration. Foxy approves of him completely. She insists that he is right for her and that she loves her husband. Yet she betrays him. Piet who "loved any woman he lay with" (336) and who is easily persuaded, tries to avoid a repetition of the affair with Foxy after the birth of Ken's child. Admitting that sexual gratification is greater with her husband, Foxy nevertheless lures Piet into a resumption of an affair which can end only in disaster. Foxy Whitman is complexity embodied in a beautiful woman.

Piet's wife, Angela, is another Updike complexity. The most admired and respected of the ten women in the magic circle, she is the one who, before the end of the story, behaves most inconsistently. She is an aristocrat who believes "nothing" (20) but whose standards of morality are at first beyond reproach. She is concerned for the neglected children in her social set and disapproves of the drunkenness and foul language at the parties of their friends. She doesn't express a "holier than thou" attitude toward the others but tells her husband that *she* feels dirty after one of their parties. She thinks there is something wrong with the way they all live. Foxy, while sleeping with Angela's husband, describes her as "gracious and careless and above it all at the same time" (74). Foxy looks up to Angela who is in a "luxurious detached realm where observations and impressions [drift] nodding by one another like strolling aristocrats" (59). Suspecting that her husband has more than one bed to sleep in, Angela says she doesn't want to know about his women. Perhaps her self-deception is a way of protecting herself, and perhaps it is a means of release from responsibility, for when he needs her most, she cannot be reached. In one scene when he desperately wants her to listen to him, to know his troubles and to allow his confession, she serenely refuses him because she is absorbed in the make believe of a novel. At other times she has the patience, the forgiving spirit of a saint. She even finds fault with herself, confessing her own inadequacies, deciding that it is her suspicious nature and not disloyalty of Piet that makes her think he is having affairs with other women. Even when he is caught in a lie, she ignores it because she wants to believe in him.

There is one incident involving Angela which is so inconsistent it goes beyond the realm of plausibility, even in such a complex person as Piet's wife. She is highly moral. She has had no extramarital affairs even though several of the men are wistful and frequently propose such to her. Piet is forced, as a part of his bargain in obtaining an abortion for Foxy, to ask his wife to sleep with the man most disdained by the members of the group. Unhesitatingly, she agrees. She doesn't even ask what the bargain is. She just quietly accommodates her husband's associate without complaint. This does not seem to be the act of the Angela the reader knows, no matter how complex she is. It is impossible to reconcile the incident to her nature. Had she been in the habit of serving her husband out of love or even out of some exaggerated concept of duty, such conduct might be plausible, but she is the same woman who is often too busy reading to serve him as a companion and wife. She is the woman who detests the sex games of the crowd. The illusion of reality is completely destroyed when she complacently accepts an arrangement in which her husband literally sells her services to pay off a debt. Piet and Foxy are complex. Angela is unbelievable. Together with other members of their Tarbox circle, they forcefully if unconvincingly illustrate the Updike theme of the complexity of human personality.

Whether lonely, confused, or complex, almost every member of the social group is a searcher. The theme of man in search of God or, less specifically, of man searching, may be a part of or a function of nearly every serious novel of note in contemporary American writing. It is present in some degree in every Updike novel. Reduced from the search for Good, God, and Identity in the earliest Updike novels to sex fulfillment in *Of the Farm*, the transition novel, the topic recurs in *Couples* with new impact. The search, altered in dimension and scope, is increased in intensity.

Piet searches for an ultimate comfort—not for God. He behaves as though God stands by and waits for him to find something to satisfy his ever-present, instinctive hungers and will, when Piet is satisfied, take him by the hand and lead him gently on. For Piet God is not absent; He just doesn't figure very strongly in the current scheme of things. Like Harry Angstrom of *Rabbit, Run*, Piet searches for *something*, which, because he doesn't try to define it, takes the form of sexual fulfillment. Since sex is an appetite ever renewed and varied, there is no fulfillment. His search will continue with him into old age where, undefined and unfulfilled, it will die with him.

Foxy's search is, initially, for someone to be recipient

of her gifts of self. Her husband could have answered her need and enjoyed her gift, but he is "wilfully ignorant, hollow and afloat" (68). To him the sharing of a house, a view, and a carefully arranged marriage is adequate. His search is for personal recognition among intellectuals whom he imitates but with whom he cannot compete. He is unaware of any need other than his own. Recognizing that Ken will never return her kind of warmth, that she will not in him find her needs fulfilled, Foxy turns to the first responsive man she knows who is as unrestrained as she is. At this point her search becomes an unquenchable thirst. Her offering of self is quickly transformed into impatient self-indulgence, for, like Piet's, her need is increased but never satisfied. She thinks of God and the world "as the same" (203), reducing God to a conveniently flexible and permissive entity. He doesn't interfere with her conduct by imposing a conscience upon her. Her God, like Piet's, waits patiently on the sidelines. Her search will not end with her second husband, for a change of husbands is not what she had sought. Like Piet, she searches without knowing what she seeks, and, like Piet's, her search, unfulfilled, will die with her.

The search in *Couples* is much broader than that illustrated through Piet and Foxy, however. The circle of twenty people at the pinnacle of Tarbox society illustrates man's perpetual longing which is not satisfied by arrival in utopia. For they have all that is usually considered necessary for contentment. For the most part, they have all the consumer goods they need. Each couple enjoys an adequate or a luxurious home, a secure income, freedom from financial worries. They have normally healthy or even superior and beautiful children. Treasured friendships enrich their lives. Most of them are well-educated and enjoy the esthetics of art and music —at least on the looking and listening level. Shakespeare is a familiar topic of discussion. French occasionally punctuates their conversations with a flourish. The mysteries of science are cocktail talk among several of the men. All are reasonably knowledgeable people.

Several of them feel certain responsibilities toward society in general, creating local issues so that they can have something on which to spend their time, but none allows truly serious social or political problems to disturb his peace of mind. They are comfortably detached from the world. Giving the story reality by linking it here and there with historical events, the author arranges for one of the couples to have a party on the date of John F. Kennedy's assassination. A few of the individuals express some doubt as to the propriety of a party during a time of national mourning, but all respond to the rationalization of the hostess that they can feel "terrible together" and that the party can be "an Irish wake, and a formal dinner-dance . . . for the dead man, who had had such style" (295). They are people who allow little to interfere with their pleasures. Their way of life approaches a modern utopia.

Accordingly, they insist on few restraints among themselves. They are permissive and forgiving. Two of the couples, the Smiths and the Applebys, see so much of one another and enjoy each other's company so unreservedly that it is eventually as easy to trade wives as it is to trade recipes. One of the wives is a little harder to placate than the other, but even she accepts the consoling delights of the bed of her friend's husband. The "Applesmiths" as these four are appropriately dubbed, set the patterns of tolerance and generosity which the others follow. Morality is a relative thing and proves to be merely consciousness of being watched by other couples. That not discovered is not immoral, and if discovered, is easily forgiven. Each couple, aware of what another is doing, takes care not to be seen nor to see, and few moral issues arise.

With few restraints and a mutually acceptable amoral code, members of the group have little need of God. Or at least they think they have little need of Him. Most of them have given up the idea that there is a God—at least one who has a meaning for them personally. Even Piet and Foxy who profess some belief accept the patterns of behavior of the nonbelievers. Their belief has little effect on their conduct. Amorality is a part of affluent comfort.

But with all their self-sufficiency and open-mindedness, the ten couples of Tarbox are still seekers. The very fact of their dissatisfaction with one another and their exchanges of marriage partners is symptomatic of their need. They "have everything" but are not satisfied. There is hardly a weekend when any one couple is content to enjoy their home and children, their own abundance and leisure. They have endless parties, a chain of intimate affairs, one linking with and causing the next. Even the organized games played at their parties reflect their ceaseless search for something—something.

"Wonderful" is a game which the group invents. When eating, drinking, and sex games are exhausted, they play "wonderful." There is nothing in the book which illustrates more vividly the pitiful plight of these people. They are intelligent individuals with the potential of artists and poets. They can see and appreciate beauty; they are sensitive to the nuances of emotion and deep feelings. But instead of using their talents creatively, they substitute a game which will be forgotten with the next drink or a new sex partner. In "wonderful" each person simply names the most marvelous thing he can think of. After much talk and many digressions on a particular evening, the sum of wonderful things is produced: a baby's fingernails, a sleeping woman, Bach, the Eucharist, the stars, the human capacity for self-deception.

Tenderness, beauty, emotion, depth of feeling, awe,

intelligent thought—all traits of the potentially remarkable, are witnessed in these individuals, but unhappily, they make little use of their talents except to entertain one another. There are no ultimates, only contests. They complete one game only to find need for a new form of entertainment, a new self-indulgence. The fruits of their efforts are without substance. A new weekend will bring another party, another game, another try at enjoying life but no fulfillment. Their abilities to feel, to appreciate, to think are exploited for the sake of fun. Nothing is found. The search continues.

Directly and indirectly the author of *Couples* suggests that these twenty citizens of Tarbox and the thousands of Americans they represent involuntarily search for something because they have not found God. They have everything else. A familiar Updike theme takes shape: man needs a modern religion. Only a concept of God which demands the awe of sophisticated modern man will do. In a world where man is conquering the mysteries of life itself, the superstitions and nonsense of religious belief of the past (the Christian Church of the past) will not do. The Church is an outmoded vehicle; once a medium of inspiration and faith, it is no longer useful. Man needs a new religion, a new Church, a new faith which can cope with man in space, earth and satellites in orbit among orbits among orbits of the eternal universe. Change is the order of the universe and of man who changes as all things change. Man's concept of God changes as man changes. The Christian Church which met the needs of a limited number of men five centuries ago or fifty years ago is not adequate for modern society. Religion must be infallible and yet must encompass perpetual change if it is to meet the needs of modern man. Religion—man's way to God—must accommodate change and yet be impervious to change.

The author develops his thesis step by step. The first

tenet is that we cannot live in the past, for it does not exist. He illustrates this undeniable fact through several characters who would like to return to the past. Foxy Whitman frequently looks to the security of her childhood for reassurance, but the childhood and its security are gone. She tries to recall the solidity of her parents' marriage, the family unity which the three of them had known, but the parents are divorced; the marriage and family solidity no longer exist. Even the mother Foxy remembers is not available. The woman who keeps her company while she waits for the birth of her baby is not the mother of the plain, listening face of Foxy's childhood but is "Connie" who, now married to a wealthy man, is a gay, well-costumed and coiffed guest in Foxy's house. Yearn as she might, Foxy's past is gone.

Piet, too, looks backward "with the eyes of a child" (12) only to find a silent void. In his lonely separation from the society of which he is nominally a part, he dreams of the greenhouse where his parents nursed plants to bloom and spoke soft, indistinguishable Dutch to each other. He longs for the comfort of their voices. It does not come. They are gone. They were of the past which does not now exist.

The fact of the dead past established, Updike applies the same principle to the Church, our traditional home of religious expression. We cannot hope to be fortified by the Church of the past. Its comforting dogmas to which we could turn as children no longer exist as they did in the perspective of childhood. They have been negated or obliterated by change. We have changed; society has changed. The Church which was adequate in the past, though it may still exist in name, cannot meet our needs of the present. We would *like* it to, but it will not. Freddy Thorne, the tolerated but unloved member of the *Couples* circle, the most blasphemous of the group, says the Christian Church is comical. When others press him, he admits, "Christ, I'd love to believe it. . . . Any of it. Just the littlest bit of it. Just one lousy barrel of water turned into wine. Just half a barrel. A quart. I'll even settle for a pint. . . . I can't" (146).

Piet, one man who pretends that his beliefs have not changed, is really more superstitious than faithful. He is afraid not to believe. His fears and need of reassurance indicate his lack of real faith. His standard of morality which should be inseparable from his religious beliefs reflects little if any faith. He prays out of habit but admits to himself, "nobody listens" (212). He cannot reach God through a severed communication line or through a faith which does not exist.

Nearly all of the principal characters in the story reflect a yearning for something of a religious past which no longer serves. They are people who know Biblical names and stories. They use Bible quotations readily and depict Bible characters in the game of "impressions." They have the vocabulary of religious people but do not have the faith or the Church. They talk about prayer but do not pray. At a dinner party there is, instead of grace, "a brief bump of silence" (25) suggesting their wish for the comforts but awareness of the emptiness of the rituals of the past.

Even the children in the story help make the point of their dead religion. Piet's daughter, Ruth, realistically drawn, is bolder than most of the adults. Finding her father's concept of God inadequate for her needs, she declares, "God is retarded" (215). Her intelligence cannot accept her father's God. The God of a generation one step removed from her is inadequate for her needs. Unlike her father who is restrained by habit and superstition, she is free to admit her disbelief. The past is dead. God as perceived in the past has died with it.

The third level in Updike's argument regarding man's need for a *now* religion is expressed in the example of the relationship of members of the social twenty in *Couples*. They make a church of each other. Their need for a community of love is so strong that, having rejected the formal church, they create their own, complete with priest and ritual and even some ideals usually associated with organized religion. Their "church" does not lead them to God, for they are not searching for God. They are searching for something to take His place. They are trying to *create* a god, not to find *the* God. They want a convenient god of their making, not the universal God that *is*.

Herein, Updike seems to suggest, lies their failure and that of perhaps many much more sophisticated churches. Here is the key to the need for change. God does not change, but man's limited image of Him does. It must, for it is always inadequate; it is always man's idea of God, not God's revelation of Himself. Man foolishly rejects *Him* when he can no longer accept the limited image created out of his own limited vision.

The "church" created by Tarbox couples has a priest, Freddy Thorne, the man they tolerate without loving and hear without heeding. They seek him out when they can use him but ignore him when he offers unsolicited advice. Freddy is almost aware of his role as priest. A dentist by profession, he is a self-styled psychiatrist by avocation. Early in the story he tells Angela he thinks the ten couples are "a magic circle of heads to keep the night out" and that they have "made a church of each other" (7). Updike, strengthening the priestly role for Freddy, reveals him in his dentist's garb as in "sacerdotal white" (356) and sets the view from his office window "upward over back yards toward the tip of the Congregational church" (356).

Freddy sees himself as something of a counselor. He tries, in his crude way, to give advice and sometimes makes personal sacrifices to help others. When he sees that Janet Appleby is finding the "Applesmith" spouse-trading affair distasteful, he offers to have an affair with her, as little or as much of an affair as she wants, to get her out of the mess. She knows he is really interested in another woman and can't understand his offer. He explains, simply, "I like to help people" (165).

It is a genuine threat to his career when he arranges and carries out an abortion for Foxy Whitman, but he does it because he wants to help two people he loves—in his own crude way. He demands a sacrifice from Piet as payment, the kind which requires total acquiescence of his parishioner yet one he cannot use and does not want personally. It is a sacrifice to the "establishment" and is designed to humble and totally tax the giver, not to appease a god. By demanding it, Freddy firmly establishes his infallibility as priest. He insists on a night with Piet's wife, gets it, accepts it, and then cannot glean from it any pleasure. It is not a personal reward the "priest" has demanded from Piet but a ritual sacrifice, a beloved and unspoiled lamb, a precious treasure. It is complete submission in payment for absolution.

Angela seeks out Freddy at parties to discuss children and "psychology." Janet goes to him for marriage counsel. Foxy asks him to get her an abortion. Piet asks his help in time of crisis and makes sacrificial payment, the irreplaceable gift of his wife's faithfulness. Freddy wants to serve, to listen to confessions, to demand sacrifices. He is the priest of the church he creates for his circle of friends.

Another function of the priest is to preach to his flock. Freddy preaches. One of his topics is love, another, man's purpose on earth, and another, death.

His sermons on love are repeated, revised, and delivered again and again at the weekend gatherings of his laity. Summarily, his message is that love would solve all our problems but that people do not wish to give them-

selves fully enough, that they do not love enough. "People hate love. It threatens them. It's like tooth decay, it
smells and it hurts. I'm the ony man alive it doesn't
threaten, I wade right in with pick and mirror. I love you,
all of you, men, women, neurotic children, crippled dogs,
mangy cats, cockroaches. People are the only thing people have left since God packed up" (145). The physical
aspect of love provides a favorite synonym for all levels of
love or for death or even for people in Freddy's vocabulary. With little effort he mixes them all together upon
definition. "By people I mean sex" (145).

On the topic of man's purpose on earth, Freddy says,
"I've seen the light. You know why we're all put here on
earth. . . . It just came to me. A vision. We're all put
here to humanize each other" (148). In his crass way, he
tries to help his friends "humanize" one another. But
humanizing seems also to be directly related to sex, for he
states life's purpose in another way: "You are born to get
laid and die, and the sooner the better" (242). His parishioners make every effort to fulfill his second definition
of purpose—except for the dying part.

Death gives Freddy his most frequent sermon topic.
He recognizes everyone's fear of death and does what he
can to help them dispel it, but unskilled as he is, he
usually increases the fear. He explains that people deceive themselves about staying young and that the "nifty
machine we begin with . . . runs only one way. Down-
hill" (242). Death is a part of living. "We don't die for
one second out there in the future, we die all the time,
in every direction" (370). He is of no particular comfort
to his listeners when he launches into this, one of his
most perplexing topics, but he does try to say what he
thinks. He believes in little but love and death—and both
are tragic.

"I believe there are tragic things and comic things.
The trouble is, damn near everything, from the yellow

stars on to the yummy little saprophytes subdividing inside your mouth, are tragic" (146). And relating love, tragedy, death, and God, he directs each stream into his favorite channel of thought, sex. Never able to separate sex from any of his theories, he explains God and death in familiar terms. "Death excites me. Death is being screwed by God. It'll be delicious" (370). When challenged that he doesn't believe in God, he says, "I believe in that one, Big Man Death" (370).

The group which has made a church of itself has a priest, and it has rituals. Appropriately, meetings are held at least once a week, usually on Saturday and Sunday, for the parties which begin with the setting of the sun on Saturday continue into the early hours of Sunday, and, after a pause in which members succumb to sleep, resume in the late afternoon. Encompassing both Saturday and Sunday, they can accommodate either preference for a Sabbath and do include members who are at least nominally Protestant, Catholic, Jewish, and, originally, of some ancient Oriental religion. There are no prejudices in the decadent church. Rituals include games of fellowship of kindred souls of a variety of cultures, gestures of love, "sermons" by the priest, eating and drinking, and confession. Games of "impressions" and "wonderful" are actually rituals for probing into one another's secrets and innermost thoughts. Like inquisitors, they examine and cross-examine each other. Relentlessly, they catechize and question. Every week each member is tried, found guilty, forgiven, and sanctified in the eyes of all. In their own way, they are a community of the concerned, serving and comforting one another.

There are, indeed, aspects of their relationships which, out of context, exemplify the finest brotherhood. The "Applesmiths," the first two couples who exchange spouses as part of their love ritual, had managed, for a while, to practice an unusually close friendship. Their excesses of lust soon drain the affair of anything resembling camaraderie or mutual respect, and finally, as Freddy predicts, they "hate love" as well as one another. All that might have been commendable is lost.

When Foxy is recovering from the abortion of the baby Piet has fathered, a second mistress of Piet, Georgene, nurses and cares for her with genuine tenderness. In a situation where many women out of jealousy would have been more inclined to crucify a woman for having stolen a lover, Georgene forgives all and ministers to the needs of the suffering Foxy. Protecting her secret, keeping her company, restoring her to health, Georgene is almost saintly in her loyalty to her sister-in-love. She is one member of the group who knows love on more than one level. It cannot last, however, for Foxy sacrifices her new friendship for the sake of a return to her sex partner. Nothing, not friendship, not life itself is valued as highly as the sexual relationship. Freddy's parishioners are devoted to their cause. They live "to get laid."

As the characters in *Couples* are gentle and tolerant of each other, so their creator is gentle and tolerant of them. Any criticism of their way of life must be made by the reader. The author tells about them as they are, at one moment loving or youthfully beautiful, at another foolish, dissipated, depraved. He describes them; he does not pass judgment on them.

They bring about their own judgment in the forcing of events which they could have avoided. A quotation from Alexander Blok's "The Scythians" serves as a prologue to the book and an explanation of the certainty of the punishment they will suffer.

> We love the flesh: its taste, its tones,
> Its charnel odor, breathed through Death's jaws. . . .
> Are we to blame if your fragile bones
> Should crack beneath our heavy, gentle paws?

He does not say through Blok that their love of flesh is sin, but he does say that it preludes its own defeat. Call it what we may, "sin" or just "behavior," that conduct which serves only the selfish will of the flesh leads to chaos. In society selfish conduct of any kind will not be limited in its effects to the performer. Solitary actions are not possible. Everything one does in a society of two or more people is felt by or influences others. Foxy Whitman thinks Tarbox has taught her how to play the game of "tempting fate," but once she learns the rules, she is an expert and herself an instructor of inestimable skill.

Another prologue to *Couples* quotes one of modern theology's outstanding spokesmen, Paul Tillich, a philosopher to whom Updike refers frequently in his published works.

There is a tendency in the average citizen, even if he has a high standing in his profession, to consider the decisions relating to the life of the society to which he belongs as a matter of fate on which he has no influence —

But each man's conduct does have an influence on society. What he does and what he thinks eventually bring about the "decisions relating to the life of the society to which he belongs." Or at least this seems to be what Updike is revealing to us through *Couples*.

Behavior of one is imitated by another and another. Group behavior makes its own decisions and determines the rules for society. Georgene Thorne, having an affair with Piet Hanema, worries for fear her husband will have one with Janet Appleby. Piet tells her that Freddy is "naughty," and she replies, "Maybe he is because I am. Because we are" (90). Janet Appleby, discovering that her husband is sleeping with Marcia Smith, decides she has a right to seek the company of Harold Smith. Her husband's conduct has influenced hers; her conduct will influence Harold's. The behavior of the four of them sets a pace for that of sixteen other people. Influence multiplies and grows, doubling upon itself many times over.

The Smiths of the "Applesmith" foursome are frequently called the "little Smiths" because, at the top of the social register, they have taken the place formerly held by another Smith couple whose social cortege, once prominent, has disbanded. The new elite rise to prominence with the new Smiths out of the well-fertilized setting, flourish for a brief time, indulge in extramarital sex, engorge themselves on lust, sicken, and enrich the ground of influence with their own disintegration. A new, younger crowd sprouts quickly, promising to repeat the example of the "couples."

It is not fate that makes the decisions for society. Each man decides upon his own behavior; his decision influences another; his imitator sets an example for still another: One man's mistake germinates flowering chaos. The eventual death of the plant is its own punishment which is certain for the individual and for society. Most of the couples seem to understand the behavioral cycle but their knowledge does not deter them from selfish living. Harold Smith, contemplating adultery with Janet Appleby, comments, "We'll all be punished no matter how it goes. That's a rule of life" (136).

Sin in a traditional sense, the disobedience of the ecclesiastical law, is not the topic of the novelist. He shows us people behaving: responding, loving, reacting, hating. Perhaps their errors—or sins—can be summed up in one sin: separating themselves from God.

Updike lets us see people who are intent upon living abundantly, not on sinning. They are capable of love, forgiveness, goodness, sacrifice. Why, then, does their way of life fail? The key seems to be in the fact that they put self, not God, at the center of things. Perhaps this, after all, is the worst of sins. Paul Tillich, whose philosophy has evidently been of some influence on Updike, offers a clue in *The Eternal Now*, the book from which the *Couples* prologue is quoted. "Sin is our act of turning away from participation in the Divine Ground from which we come and to which we go. Sin is the turning towards ourselves, and making ourselves the center of our world and of ourselves." [4] Members of the *Couples* society certainly turn away from all things divine. They clearly focus on themselves and place self at the center of everything. They make a church of themselves, paying tribute to their senses, to their bodies, to lust, not to any being or essence beyond themselves. Since, from a Tillich and evidently an Updike point of view, they exclude God, they sin.

The definition of sin once established as the separation from God, a familiar Bible phrase readily follows: "The wages of sin is death." (Romans 6:23) The death theme receives significant emphasis in all Updike fiction and is not slighted in *Couples*. Fear of death torments several of the individuals portrayed in this, Updike's most complex novel to date. Freddy's discussions of the topic reveal his dread and reflect that of others, but Piet is the one through whom the author most forcefully illustrates man's fear of eternal death.

Death for Piet is sometimes such an ordinary thing that it occurs "on the same plane as birth and marriage and the arrival of the daily mail" (428) —at least when it is someone else's death. As he sits at the bedside of a friend whose death is imminent, Piet feels nothing more than an intense awareness of sea and sun and shells and sand dollars—such is the impact of another man's death. The experience does little more than make him appreciate, momentarily, the life he still possesses.

At other times awareness of death is acute for Piet, particularly when he looks at life's smallest creatures with a sense of kinship. Updike frequently reveals another Tillich concept through Piet, the man who notices death in little things. "Man is rooted in the same ground as all things in the universe."[5] Piet sees himself as a small part of that universe, dying a little as each fragment of it dies. The death of his daughter's pet hamster and his task of burying it give cause for fearful thoughts. He sees human likeness in the little corpse and parallels its death with his own. He sees spring's "slow thronging of growth" at the edge of the woods where he buries the animal as a "tangled hurrying toward death" (78). A common symbol for life and rebirth, spring spells instead, for Piet, certain, repetitious, eternal death for all things including himself.

He envies a child he sees playing nonchalantly with pebbles in the driveway of the funeral home, "growing up in odor of embalming oil instead of flowers" (81). Such a child will perhaps be spared a fear of death. During a party at his own house where all others are experiencing the joy of living, he leaves his guests and goes to the bedsides of his daughters to listen to the fragility of life whispered in their breathing. He is constantly listening for death and trying to reassure himself with the fact that life is still present for him and those he loves.

Such a fear is, of course, reflected in his children. Nancy, about five years old, wants proof of her father's heaven, wants to go there to see the dead hamster, and at one time declares, "I will never grow up and I will never in my whole life die" (14). Piet sees that he "represent[s] death" (348) to his child but cannot seem to alter the fact no matter how he tries to reassure her.

Terrified by its certainty, he dwells on death. He frequently recalls the highway accident of his parents, allowing his imagination to recreate the last horrible moments for them and reliving every detail of the events following the crash. For Piet "the world wore a slippery surface" (19) like that of the highway on which his parents had skidded to their deaths. When he prays for them, he always wanders to thoughts about the certainty that he, too, will die. When he watches his daughter singing in the church choir, his unvoiced sensation is that "death leaned above him like a perfectly clear plate of glass" (20). He talks to his mistress about death. He dreams about it.

Certain of death for all things including himself, and terrified of it, he nevertheless is fascinated by its variety, imagining, during fits of insomnia, the details of dozens of kinds of tortures.

The Chinese knife across the eye. . . . The commando's piano wire. The crab in the intestine. The chicken bone in the windpipe. . . . The rotting kidney turning the skin golden. The shotgun blast purging the skull of brains. The massive coronary. The guillotine. The frayed elevator cable. The booming crack and quick collapse of ice. . . . The threshing machine. The random shark. Puffy-tongued dehydration. Black-faced asphyxia. Gentle leprosy. Crucifixion. Disembowelment. Fire. Gas in the shower room. The scalper's hurried adze. . . . The pull of the rack. The suck of the sea. The lion's kittenish gnawing. The loose rock, the slipping boot, the dreamlike fall. . . . The bullet, the bomb, the plague, the wreck. (259)

Like an acrophobiac who fears heights but is tempted to leap off the cliff, Piet seems impelled to think about death, even to welcome it.

Even though he fears it, death seems an easy solution to his problems. He and a friend play golf on the day in 1962 when President Kennedy holds his own against Khrushchev over Cuba. Believing that Russia will drop bombs on the United States rather than submit to inspection at the blockade, Piet now and then glances at the sky for the enemy bombers. He is happy, relieved. Soon his problems will vanish with him. When his car radio announces that the Russians have submitted to inspection, he feels disappointment that he must go on.

Now he must continue to await death. To have had it over once and for all would have been a relief.

At one time he dreams of a death plunge in a sleek, new jet airplane. Dreaming, he is tranquil, undisturbed, ready to die, but when he wakes to find himself in his own bedroom, he cannot "reenter the illusion of security" (256) of his surroundings. Awake and sleeping he wishes to die. The anticipation of dying is more fearful than death itself; in such anticipation he must live and suffer. Death would be luxuriously sweet.

And yet Piet's preoccupation with death is a direct result of his fear that he will be punished eternally. After his dream of dying in the fall of the great jet, he tries to pray but his "up-pouring thoughts touched nothing" (257). He cannot reach God. He wants to be forgiven but no one hears his supplications. Instead, he hears within himself the words of repeated Bible lessons. "Thou shalt not covet. Whosoever lusteth in his heart" (257). He flagellates himself with the thought that he has "patronized his faith and lost it. God will not be used. Death stretch[es] endless under him" (257). It is eternal death which stretches "endless under him," and he tries vainly to punish himself in a hope of avoiding God's wrath. Having been nourished on the admonishments of the Calvinist church, he suffers more than those who have easily shed a less fundamental training. Had sin had no definition, punishment for sin would have been limited to its own results, but Piet knows he has sinned and suffers the fear of the damned: that he will be eternally punished and forgotten by God. Through him another Paul Tillich concept is clearly illustrated: ". . . in the depth of the anxiety of having to die is the anxiety of being eternally forgotten."[6] Piet Hanema is afraid he will die forever and be forever forgotten.

As significant as it is in *Couples*, the subject of fear of death is not given the attention devoted to the third of life's "three great secret things": sex. It has not been possible to discuss art and religion independently of sex as they have been used here, and it may seem there could be little more to note about the third of Updike's *Couples* themes, but a few important things remain to be said about the topic and the book with which Updike has taken a bold leap into the mainstream of best-selling novels.

The fact that a novelist with the integrity and depth of John Updike has expended the effort necessary to write four hundred and fifty pages of disciplined prose about the sex encounters of twenty people suggests something more than a determination to reach the best seller lists though that goal can hardly have been overlooked. His effort suggests that sex *is* important to write about. It suggests that as one of the factors which give our lives purpose and continuity it *ought* to be written about. *Couples* is not a sneak preview or a lewd floor show. It is a book about an undeniable force in society, the force which perpetuates life. Sex is hardly new. It is as old as breathing and as essential. It is as vital to us as religion. It is as expressive as art and more creative. It is human kind relating instinctively to the forces of the universe of which we are a part; sex cannot easily be omitted from an honest account of human activity. Updike writes about sex without apology.

Couples is essentially a story of twenty people, but it is also a story about American society today. In no way does the author say that *all* America is like the Applebys and the Whitmans and the Smiths, but in several ways he does say that many Americans are.

Tarbox is a typical American town. The shops and landmarks are so familiar the reader knows where to stop for a cup of coffee and just how to bypass traffic quickly to reach the freeway. There is nothing very remarkable about it yet nothing so seriously out of order but that it can be corrected by the town's politically ambitious. It is a comfortable place where affluence rules but where there are no millionaires and no one going hungry. It is like thousands of towns to be found on the map. Janet Appleby says, "I think we're the prettiest unselfconscious town in America" (31) which is what a loyal citizen always says about his hometown. Tarbox is twenty-five miles from Boston or some other American city. It represents Smalltown, U.S.A.

The citizens we meet are not particularly unusual, either. They happen to be of the age group and the financial level of whom the men have "stopped having careers and the women . . . having babies. Liquor and love are left" (12), but that they have stopped having purpose in life would not occur to them. Their purpose is to live abundantly. Though most of them can afford luxurious living, they do not belong to country clubs and have no servants. The Applebys and the Smiths have a "modest determination to be free, to be flexible and decent" (106). The twenty Tarbox citizens are real residents of Smalltown, U.S.A.

The one factor which excludes them from representing all affluent, flexible, nonreligious people of Smalltown is their sex life. Angela Hanema calls Tarbox a "sexpot" (210). Georgene Thorne welcomes Piet to "post-pill paradise" (91). That the group is "decent" as the Applebys and the Smiths consider themselves is a matter of opinion. It is reasonable, however, to suggest that the ten couples do represent a significant percentage of Americans. The game of "switcheroo" or wife-swapping is commonly known. If one can judge by the "advice-to-the-mixed-up" columns in American newspapers and several not too unprofessional reports in print, the practice of exchanging spouses on an organized basis, even in clubs where rules are strict, is as common as headache. The people we meet in *Couples* are not as bold as organized switcheroo players and are possibly even more common. They make their trades—at least for a while—surreptitiously. Unlike members of many swapping clubs, they do suffer guilt feelings and do not feel free of society's restrictions on their behavior. They represent real Americans, how many it would be impossible to guess.

Piet Hanema, the person around whom most of the action in *Couples* centers, is also a representative figure. The reader will always remember him as an Updike individual, but he's remarkably familiar. His features are "pricked from underneath by an acquired American something—a guilty humorous greed, a wordless question" (3). We know people like him, searchers without compass or map, knowing not what they seek nor why, appeasing greedy appetites only by the promise of feasting again and soon.

Like millions of other Americans, Piet and his Tarbox friends have more leisure than they know how to use and find that partying is the logical way to spend it. The next stage, after the gatherings become tiresome, is sex experiments on the part of one or two of the least inhibited. An "affair" is just a way to add excitement to life. The behavior is contagious since moral and religious commitments are not strong. From the relationships that result, some of them suffer severe emotional conflicts, but most of them are able to save their marriages. Two divorces result.

One mistake the Tarbox friends make is a common one with Americans—perhaps with people everywhere. They think of love as synonymous with sex. They are intelligent enough to discriminate between the two, to know that love can include or be free of sex and that sex can exist alone, but they make little effort at distinction. They have a warm, friendly feeling—a degree of love—for one another. It is easy to go to bed with one another. When Frank Appleby suggests that Jesus Christ's advice to love one's neighbor is unsound biologically, Janet reminds him, "He said love, He didn't say lay your neighbor" (140). But even Janet forgets the difference when the occasion is ripe. Generalizing about her, the author tells us "We move from birth to death amid a crowd of others and the name of the parade is love" (157). What the couples seem to forget is that expressions of love can be made in ways other than acts of copulation.

One explanation for the Tarbox socialites' inability to distinguish between love in general and sex in particular is the same trait which leads them astray in their religious quest—selfishness. They want to live freely. To them freedom means doing as one pleases, having what one wants. They are in the habit of having what they want. When the idea occurs to one of them to take a bed partner other than spouse, he takes the partner as he would a second piece of pie. Calling greed "love" makes it less gross and helps to justify the act in the mind of the selfish performer. In love there can be self*less* restraints. In sex without love there is an insatiable appetite, a hunger never filled. Piet learns his mistake too late. He thinks he loves each mistress, but after losing Angela and their children because of lust, he realizes that what he has left is sex without love, and though somewhat reluctant to give up the family he loves, he recognizes that the force of sex in his own life is stronger than that of love. He prefers sex without love to love without sex. "Sex is like money; only too much is enough" (437).

A second reason for the confusion in which Piet and Foxy, particularly, find themselves seems to be the fault of society and its limitations upon people who, loving and passionate, are pledged for a lifetime to partners who do not return love and passion of an equal degree. Love and sex thrive on love and sex returned, and a passionate partnership is impossible when one spouse is cold and unresponsive. Society demands an unreasonable sacrifice when it insists that once pledged always pledged, regardless of the success of sex in a marriage. The story suggests no solutions; it simply describes the difficulties in which such people are trapped. Piet and Foxy need to be loved as they love. Because they are not thus loved by their marriage partners, they seek fulfillment outside the marriage bed, both admitting continued love for their spouses. Modern society makes it impossible for the Piets and Foxys to satisfy the sex appetite with anyone other than the marriage partner, no matter how frigid, without suffering punishment.

They both know that because of their social and religious inheritance they will exercise self-punishment as well. Their relationship takes on a pathetic quality because of this knowledge. Piet, not entirely understanding it, describes to his wife his affair with Foxy as "religious somehow, and sad" (393). Foxy, in a similar vein, tells him, after divorce proceedings have begun, that "lovemaking [is] an exploration of a sadness so deep people must go in pairs, one cannot go alone" (451). Both seem to realize that their relationship is sad because it is not acceptable to society and that since it is not, the two of them, part of that society, cannot be entirely happy.

The case Updike presents is that man puts sex first—uppermost—above all things, above other aspects of love, above religion. He puts sex above God or makes a god of sex, limiting himself thereby to only a part of God, only a part of love. At the same time, man claims paradoxically through his moral laws that sex is evil except in very limited situations between marriage partners. Allowing sex to rule his feelings while condemning it as largely evil, man hopelessly flounders in his own contradictions.

The most artful and appropriate symbol in *Couples* is introduced early in the narration and returns to bring the story to a conclusion. When we first read about the town, we learn that "a golden rooster turned high above

Tarbox" and that the Congregational church "lifted well over one hundred feet into the air a gilded weather-cock" (16). The discerning reader may detect its significance from the first glimpse of the cock which "deposed once each generation by hurricanes, lightning, or repairs, . . . was always much bent and welded, restored" (16–17). *Above* the pinnacle of the church steeple, *above* the religious edifice, a rooster, the boastful male fowl which traditionally crows of its sex exploits, swaggers in the wind. He has held sway in the same position through the coming and going of four religious meeting houses and many generations of Tarbox citizens. Nothing has displaced him in prominence. Nothing has been given the same attention. Even the "children in the town grew up with the sense that the bird was God. That is, if God were physically present in Tarbox, it was in the form of this unreachable weathercock visible from everywhere" (17). The cock is supreme. Sex, elevated above all else, is God, "physically present."

Toward the end of the story, the Congregational church is struck by "God's own lightning" (441) and burns to the ground. The church, tangible evidence of religious devotion, is vulnerable, is destructible, but even through the spirals of smoke, the crowd can see the weathercock poised securely atop the ironwork which does not burn. Firmly the cock has perched for generations. Firmly he continues to stand, golden, proud, untouched by God's own holocaust.

When the fire is out and the charred ruins are being leveled by bulldozers, as the story of religion and sex comes to an artistic conclusion, the school children are permitted a holiday to watch the rescue of the cock. A young man, glimmering in the sun "like the golden bird" (457), is hoisted by crane to the pinnacle of the building's skeleton from which, amidst the cheers of the children, he lifts the icon and carries it to safety. The little ones have had an object lesson which they will never forget: The golden rooster has survived all. They will surely follow in the ways of their parents, revering the cock above all things.

Except for a paragraph which in fashion of an epilogue tells that Piet and Foxy lived forever after but not necessarily in happiness, the story comes to an end with the ceremonious rescue of the rooster which doubtless will perch at the pinnacle of the new, modern house of worship for generations to come. Sex endures above and beyond all things.

Art, religion, and sex, and the greatest of these is sex — in Smalltown, U.S.A., at least. With the art of genius, John Updike writes *Couples* in a startlingly new manner about familiar topics. Upper middle-class Americans with everything to live for are lonely, confused, and fearful of death. Like all mankind, they continue to search for something; unlike a few, they do not seek God. They search for an ultimate which will comfort and accommodate them, one which will remove burdens of guilt and responsibility, one which will require little or nothing in return. They want a god who is entirely permissive, who loves but does not punish, who provides but does not require tribute.

In other words, they do not try to find God but to *make* God. Having found their parents' concept of God inadequate for their needs, they decide that it is God who is inadequate or that there is no God. Instinctively in the loneliness which results, they seek comfort from one another. Their longing for the assurance of a faith in *something* creeps into their games and their conversations until they establish rituals which roughly parallel religious worship. Since to them "sex" and "love" are synonymous, they have altered only slightly the Christian concept that God is love. Their god is sex.

Allowing their instincts to guide them, they try to appease the sex appetite which, because sex is only *one* facet of love, does not satisfy their need. Updike's point of view seems to be that having separated themselves from God who is *complete* love, these people suffer the automatic punishment of unfulfilled lives, loneliness, and fear of death. Only God who does exist can comfort them.

The author's repeated assurance that God exists is renewed in *Couples*. One of the men, Ben Saltz, of Jewish origin, insists that the complex structures of biochemistry and metaphysics couldn't arise spontaneously out of chaos. He thinks it is "ridiculous for religious people to be afraid of the majesty and power of the universe" (72). He believes in God. Ben is the one of the group who, after experimenting with amoral living, returns to a God-respecting way of life and to happiness. There is some hope for his future.

For Piet Hanema, there seems to be no hope, however. Ironically, he is the one through whom the author most forcefully asserts both God's existence and man's impudence toward his Maker. Piet never argues God even within himself. God is present in the forces of nature, in Piet's anxieties, in his loves. Like a child who fears an adult might be watching when he does something forbidden, Piet prepares for an act of adultery with Georgene and asks, "Won't we embarrass God?" (54) He is also cognizant of God's planning when he thinks his body "a maze of membranes [which] never could have evolved from algae unassisted. God gave us a boost" (311). Piet knows God but does not honor Him.

Another evidence of Piet's knowledge of God is his habit of prayer. Fearing that God doesn't always listen, he nevertheless prays. Prayer is "an unsteady state of mind for him" (18), a part of his conscious and subconscious thinking. When he feels God has heard, he seems "for intermittent moments, to be in the farthest corner of a deep burrow, a small endearing hairy animal curled up as if to hibernate. In this condition he [feels] close to a massive warm secret" (18). He doesn't rationalize about God; he just exists in God's omnipresence—not intelligently, not reasonably, not graciously, but intuitively, *knowingly*. In everything—his children, the flowers in the marshes, the sex act, the shadows, the anxieties, in life and in death—God exists. Somewhat in the way that Harry Angstrom, the moral derelict of *Rabbit, Run*, attests God's presence, so Piet Hanema, the simple, errant, selfish man who wears on his chest, symbolically, a "cruciform blazon of amber hair" (7), proves God. He is a child of God.

A disobedient child, like millions of Americans, he knows God as loving father yet, through selfishness, turns from Him. While watching the destruction of his church, the house where he has been at home with God, Piet picks up a soaked pamphlet which with a few artifacts has been saved from the fire. He reads from a sermon dated 1795.

It is the indispensable duty of all the nations of the earth, to know that the LORD he is God, and to offer unto him sincere and devout thanksgiving and praise. But if there is any nation under heaven, which hath more peculiar and forcible reasons than others, for joining with one heart and voice in offering up to him these grateful sacrifices, the United States of America are that nation. (443)

A long-forgotten minister speaks. Piet and people like him, the couples and Americans like them have forgotten to offer God "sincere and devout thanksgiving and praise." They have ceased to know God. America, if any nation under heaven, has reason to rejoice and to acknowledge God. The message is as clear and as appropriate as it was in 1795, but it goes unheeded. God exists. America wastes. The church dies. The cock lives on in glory.

8

The Short Stories

Consideration of John Updike's short stories is placed at the end of this study not because of chronological sequence (publication dates of the collections range from 1959 to 1966) but because Updike reaches his highest range of accomplishment in this medium. In the short stories he presents all of his major themes with intensity and artistic discipline more refined than that of his novels, with poetry more eloquent than that in "The Great Scarf of Birds," and with religious *empressement* to compare with that of the Psalms. In 1963 Guerin La Course said, "His most telling work thus far has been his short stories. . . . One feels that Updike has nowhere else to go in this medium, whether in form, style or resource: he has come full term." [1] Indeed it seemed he had even as early as 1963, but in the four published collections, *The Same Door* (1959), *Pigeon Feathers* (1962), *Olinger Stories* (1964), and *The Music School* (1966), and in numerous selections which have appeared month after month in widely read periodicals, Updike, through a wealth of situations, characters, and points of view, has artistically examined the problems of the individual in relation to his fellows, has enriched our scope of acquaintance with fictional persons, and, more specifically, has continued his search for a faith adequate for the contemporary thinking man.

As varied and numerous as are the characters in the short stories, there is one figure, almost an Updike stereotype, which appears again and again. He is young (either a boy or a young man), sensitive, aware of people and their complexities, responsive to nature, curious, and intelligent. He is often lonely, awkward, and misunderstood. He is an "outsider" in that as a unique individual he cannot find his place in established social coteries. His name is either David, Alan, Bill, Mark, or, most often, John. It would be easy to identify "John" of the short stories as Updike himself, but of course it is not entirely fair to do so. In any event, it seems safe to say that "John" is a character with whom Updike identifies either emotionally, physically, mentally, or in more obscure ways.

The author says of the younger "John" in the foreword to *Olinger Stories:*

He wears different names and his circumstances vary, but he is at bottom the same boy, a local boy. . . . The locality is that of Olinger, Pennsylvania . . . audibly a shadow of "Shillington," the real name of my home town, yet the two towns, however similar, are not at all the same. Shillington is a place on the map and belongs to the world; Olinger is a state of mind, of my mind, and belongs entirely to me.[2]

In many ways "John" of the Updike stories is typical of characters created by "post modern" novelists whose true subject is "the recurrent search . . . for personal identity and freedom" [3] in the complex society of post-World War II. Yet John remains uniquely Updike's creation. Unlike Salinger's Holden Caulfield, who is emotionally destroyed by the complex and crushing society of America in the 1950s, John remains cool, expectant, and sane. Unlike James Baldwin's young men, angry victims of modern society which both creates and destroys them, John of Updike's short stories is gentle, hopeful, loving, and optimistic. His moral judgment and standards of behavior would be acceptable in the most particular circles. He loves life and is conscious of its precious moments and its exquisite details. In his thoughts he often lives in the past, where there was something valuable which seems lost to the present, but he is always ready for the future, eager for its answers, anxious to be taught. He examines each new experience for its values and its hazards, taking from it a positive good even when the experience becomes a shattering one. He learns and loves and seeks answers for tomorrow, for change is certain. Disappointment is certain, but so is joy. He searches for God. In his search he listens to life and from its sobs and its songs composes a poignant melody which becomes the motif of Updike's short stories.

Nearly every published short story by Updike touches on at least one of the topics discussed here in earlier chapters, but one theme appears again and again: that of man's bewilderment as he searches for meaning in his existence. One of the stories which illustrates the complex "whorl" of man's thoughts and experiences is "Dentistry and Doubt," in which "John" is called Burton. He is a young American cleric studying at Oxford. He is a good young man making an effort to be useful and devout but finding himself a victim of doubt and confusion. His life is full of arguments against God:

> His slippers, his bathrobe, his face in the mirror, his books —black books, brown ones, C. S. Lewis, Karl Barth, *The Portable Medieval Reader*, Raymond Tully and Bertrand Russel lying together as nonchalantly as if they had been Belloc and Chesterton—stood witness to a futility that undercut all hope and theory. (*The Same Door*, 43)

While he sits in the dentist's chair, captive victim of scientific knowledge, he contemplates the questions of pride and pain, the place of the Devil in the cosmos, God's reasons for allowing the contemptuously slow process of evolution, and the unfathomable distances of time and space. He is a young modern, serious but bewildered. At the conclusion of the story, however, he reassures himself by quoting to the dentist some lines he has found in his research on the writings of Thomas Hooker, an early English Congregational clergyman: "I grant we are apt, prone, and ready, to forsake God: but is God as ready to forsake us? Our minds are changeable: is His so likewise?" (50). Man is confused. God is not. We can be comforted at least in that thought.

In "A Gift from the City," John's name is Jim, and he is a commercial artist who works and lives in New York City. A skilled and successful young man, he enjoys the comforts of a high and steady income, residence in a pleasant city apartment, and a pretty wife and a child. He is very plainly a part of the vast community of the average man. Like his peers, he loves and cares for his family, but perhaps somewhat untypically, he feels great concern for his fellowman. He is a good man, generous and thankful for life's abundance, ready at the slightest gesture to drop coins into hats of "Salvation Army singers, degraded violinists, husky blind men, . . . men noncommittally displaying their metal legs in subway tunnels" (167). For him routine follows routine in a safe, prosperous continuation of days.

Life is not that simple, however, the author seems to tell us. Perhaps a good man should live so, rewarding and being rewarded, but it cannot be so. The very fact that Jim *is* good makes him vulnerable. Beggars are not necessarily just; the needy are not always deserving; the generous are not always rewarded. A young Negro—a skilled liar and a crafty thief—learns of the man who readily gives a handout. Clever, alert, and imaginative, the beggar talks Jim and his wife out of one ten dollar bill after another until the two finally realize that they have been duped. They are victims of life as it is—not as it ought to be. The city is a place of good and evil, intermixed, inseparable. Living honestly and loving one's fellowman doesn't exempt a man from involvement in the unfathomable puzzle.]

Almost every story in John Updike's published collections illustrates the complexity of life in some way, but another emphasis is also apparent.[In the short stories as in the novel *The Centaur*, Updike tells us that goodness lives. There is always hope because man is capable of goodness. There is the young British art student in "Still Life" who refuses to pose for the vulgar American.]There is Rafe, another John who takes a plastic mobile of birds to his baby daughter in the tiny New York City apartment where one might expect to find monotony the prevailing mood. Instead, "inside his apartment, the baby had just been fed and was laughing; her mother, flushed and sleepy, lay in a slip on the sofa bed. . . . That invisible gas, goodness, stung his eyes and made him laugh, strut, talk nonsense" (66).]

In "His Finest Hour," (112) John is renamed George. He is a young intellectual who lives with his wife in a dull New York City apartment next door to a similarly dull apartment occupied by a very unintellectual couple whose name is Irva. The Irvas have an argument during which Mr. Irva attacks his wife with a kitchen knife. George and Rosalind Chandlers, living on the opposite side of a very thin wall, are obligated to call the police and are unwittingly involved in the affair. Mrs. Irva is brought into the Chandlers' apartment for treatment before being taken to a hospital. On the next day and for many weeks to follow, Mrs. Irva, restored and sober and not seriously injured, behaves as if absolutely nothing had happened. George and his wife had taken the serious risk of involvement in the bizarre affair, had befriended and aided the injured woman, even giving her one of their best blankets, which is never mentioned again. The only response from the Irvas seems to be indifference.

And then the goodness in man—even in a man like the

drunken would-be murderer, Mr. Irva—is revealed. Irva, a chef, is given all the flowers used to decorate a banquet hall where he has prepared a meal. Without a word—without even appearing on the scene—he has an entire station-wagon load of flowers delivered to the Chandlers' apartment. [Man, cruel and crude as he may be, has an occasional spark of virtue.

Illustration of the goodness of man is supported in Updike's short stories by another theme: [Life is good in little things. There are moments of joy, beauty, and insight which, even though fleeting, are as valuable in time's vast spaces as are diamonds caught here and there in the voluminous earth.] A few of the critics notice Updike's tendency to dwell on the commonplace events and the small moments of life but fail to realize the significance of this emphasis. Stanley J. Rowland, Jr., says that "John Updike devotes his energies to the small scene," [4] but he does not recognize what seems obvious—that to Updike the small scene is the key to life's greatest values. Rowland sees, instead, a writer who lacks vision and insists of Updike that "just now he is still packing a flashlight." [5] An error of judgment occurs in understanding the purpose of the "flashlight." No floodlight is needed to see things close at hand. Man is prone to overlook the obvious. Updike seems to be saying that our vision is out of perspective. We need to see the little things and to recognize their value in our lives.

There are almost innumerable illustrations of this philosophy throughout Updike's work, but some of the most forceful are found in the short stories. Ben—who is John at age ten—in "You'll Never Know, Dear, How Much I Love You," has not lost the wisdom of a child who knows where happiness is found. Ben gambles his limited allowance at a carnival, is cheated at the dart game and teased by the crowd. A man "with the stencilled arms" eventually feels guilty for taking the boy's coins one after another, and returns two of them, ordering Ben away from the board. What the adults do not understand is that Ben knows what he is doing: He is losing money, but he is living little moments of excitement; he is storing up fragments of life; "he knows his eyes are moist and his cheeks red but that's because of joy, freedom, not because of losing" (*Pigeon Feathers*, 177).

Another young man who loves the seemingly insignificant things in life and therefore has much to live for is Sammy, the narrator of "A & P," a gay story that touches ground just long enough to make the point: it is the little things that make life livable. Sammy is a check-out clerk at the A & P supermarket. When two young girls in bathing suits come through the aisles, they create a small sensation for the other customers and moments of pure delight for Sammy. Mr. Lengel, the manager, doesn't feel the same way at all. He reprimands and embarrasses the girls by telling them that "this isn't the beach. . . . We want you decently dressed when you come in here" (194). Sammy, who has appreciated their uncovered charms and who believes that life is richer for little moments such as those the girls have given him defends them verbally after their departure. The boss does not retreat, however, and Sammy, a free spirit who intends to enjoy his freedom, walks out. "I just saunter into the electric eye in my white shirt that my mother ironed the night before, and the door heaves itself open, and outside the sunshine is skating around on the asphalt" (196).

At this point the author makes a second, less carefree point. Sammy will not find life always easy. He knows "how hard the world . . . [is] going to be" (196). Perhaps he will have only a few of his little moments of certain joy, but he will have those. He is not one of the "sheep" whom Lengel checks through beside the cash register; he is a young individualist who loves life's unconventional—if infrequent—moments of excitement.

He will not always be understood, but he refuses to be captured by conformity and monotony. Updike's unspoken comment seems to be, "Sammy will live for and notice the little things, and his life will have a measure of value."

In the story, "In Football Season," of *The Music School* collection, still another "John" now grown but reminiscing about high school days, looks back at the little delights of youth which are no longer available to him: a "wasted" hour spent walking home from a ball game when a trolley would have saved time, a gentle air of permission with which his parents had surrounded him and allowed him to taste life, and even so often unnoticed a thing as a "cloudless fall sky like the blue bell of a vacuum [lifting] toward itself the glad exhalation of all things" (*The Music School*, 3). "The glad exhalation of all things" is not only something this young man recalls from his youth, it is also an Updike message. He sees glad exhalations in the minutiae, the little moments, the smallest syllables of life's voluminous treatise.

"Archangel" is an entirely different treatment of the same topic. Symbolic and elegant, it sings of Earth's delights. An archangel speaks and pays tribute to life on Earth among visible, tangible wonders. He praises warmth and color and pleasure. He sings of cold water and bronze vessels, of little things which fill our lives with comfort and joy. He says, presumably of man's lifespan on this earth, "My pleasures are as specific as they are everlasting" (*Pigeon Feathers*, 170). He lists one after another the rich treasures of tangible things, fleeting moments, and small joys which surround man and need only be possessed. Every item he names is so precious that its value can only be enjoyed, never measured. The sliced edges of a fresh ream of laid paper, cream, stiff, rag-rich. The freckles of the closed eyelids of a woman attentive in the first white blush of morning. The ball diminishing well down the broad green throat of the first at Cape Ann. The good catch, a candy sun slatting the bleachers. The fair at the vanished poorhouse. The white arms of girls dancing, taffeta, . . . music its ecstasies praise . . . the iridescence of an old copper found in the salt sand. The microscopic glitter in the ink of the letters of words that are your own. Certain moments, remembered or imagined, of childhood. (170)

When he has finished his account, the Archangel reminds us that "such glimmers I shall widen to rivers . . . the multiplication shall be a thousand thousand fold . . ." (171). No other Updike selection says more about the goodness of little things than does "Archangel." One hardly needs even a "flashlight" to find these; he needs only to open his eyes.

Updike, it seems, would have man accept life's little rewards and press on toward understanding his role and his relationship to his Creator. John of the Updike short stories is a seeker after Truth. Sometimes he is just discovering his uniqueness and hardly aware of his search. Sometimes he seeks answers in the scriptures, again in nature, and still again in mystical revelations. There is some aspect of search in almost every Updike short story. "The Happiest I've Been" is an account of John Nordholm, a young man who is ready to break the ties of childhood and home and to begin his adult life looking for something many of his schoolmates will obviously never seek. They are content with each other, with their small-town perspective, and with the prospect of a dull status quo. His is the spirit of the searcher, the young man who is happy to be on his way toward adulthood and discovery. There is no particularly religious search in this story, but John, after a final farewell to his childhood friends at an all-night teen-age party, leaves town to return to college. John realizes that life is beginning: "We were on our way. I had seen a dawn" (*The Same Door,*

241). His will be the life of the student, the searching individual, the seeker after something beyond what he already knows.

John of "The Happiest I've Been" is much like Allen
who appears in "Flight." Allen, the narrator, is seven-
teen, "poorly dressed and funny-looking . . . conscious
of a special destiny" (*Pigeon Feathers*, 49). He tells of
an event earlier in his life when he and his mother had
hiked to the top of Shale Hill overlooking the village of
Olinger, their home. There they had stood quietly for a
while, looking down at the town, and then his mother
"dug her fingers into the hair on my head and announced, 'There we all are, and there we'll be forever.'
She hesitated before the word 'forever,' and hesitated
again before adding, 'Except you, Allen. You're going to
fly' " (50). Allen is a boy apart from the crowd, a boy
who will not be content to exist through several decades
of sameness. His life will have a special significance because he will seek an understanding of his unique role.
His search will begin as soon as his mother lets him go.
At the end of the story when he has gone against her will
and has been insolent in his determination to be free, she
recognizes that his flight and his search have begun. "In
a husky voice that seemed to come across a great distance
my mother said . . . 'Goodbye, Allen' " (73).

In "Lifeguard" the narrator (who never gives his
name) is a divinity school student in the winter and a
lifeguard in the summer. During three months of the
year he perches symbolically above the crowd on the
beach, and, very much alone, ponders his role in life,
searching for meanings in the sea (and in life) "with its
multiform and mysterious hosts, its savage and senseless
rages . . . [its] immensities of blue that surround the
little scabs of land upon which we draw our lives to their
unsatisfactory conclusions" (213). The flawless metaphor expands as the young man searches books during
the winter: "I pace my pale hands and burning eyes

through immense pages of Biblical text barnacled with fudging commentary; through multivolumed apologetics couched in a falsely friendly Victorian voice" (211–12). Unconvinced of the Christian theological explanations, he nevertheless seeks through Christian sources as well as through direct observation of humanity on the beach, the solution to the puzzle of life. He is youth trying to understand, trying to save man from the dangers of the unknown, trying to discover the purpose of it all. In role of divinity student or lifeguard, he is a searcher.

A mystical search is the subject of "The Crow in the Woods," in which John appears in the role of a young father who rises on an early winter morning to care for his child. He is a sensitive man aware of the sun on the flowered wallpaper of the little girl's room, conscious of his size and the child's early-morning awe of him and of the world. As in other Updike stories, this John notices the little wonders of ordinary things. His wife's dexterity as she prepares breakfast fascinates him: "Gerber's wheat-dust came to smoke in the child's tray. Orange juice, slender as a crayon, was conjured before him" (225). And like the narrator of "The Great Scarf of Birds," he *experiences* knowledge in an incident which only the mystic seeker after Truth could understand. Through the clear window of the little rented cottage which is his home, John turns his attention to the beauty of snow in a wooded landscape.

The woods at their distance across the frosted lawn were a Chinese screen in which an immense alphabet of twigs lay hushed: a black robe crusted with white braid standing of its own stiffness. Nothing in it stirred. There was no depth, the sky a pearl slab, the woods a fabric of vision in which vases, arches, and fountains were hushed. (225)

For a brief moment his attention returns to the peculiar beauty of a warm breakfast on a gleaming plate. Then something happens.

Outdoors a huge black bird came flapping with a crow's laborious wingbeat. It banked and, tilted to fit its feet, fell toward the woods. His heart halted in alarm for the crow, with such recklessness assaulting an inviolable surface, seeking so blindly a niche for its strenuous bulk where there was no depth. It could not enter. Its black shape shattering like an instant of flak, the crow plopped into a high branch and sent snow showering from a quadrant of lace. Its wings spread and settled. The vision destroyed, his heart overflowed. "Clare!" he cried. (225–26)

John, intensely aware of Nature's beauty and awed by its splendor, studies every detail of Nature's handiwork, but for a time sees the wood and the snow as a painting, without dimension, apart from himself. He is an observer only, of something indescribably beautiful. The crow, crashing into the scene and into his consciousness, gives all a depth, reality, and meaning. John suddenly becomes a part of the scene, experiencing for a split second the awesome chasm—the height, breadth, and the unfathomable dimensions of Nature of which he and the crow are both a part. The woods, the snow, his own awareness, and the intrusion of the instinctively guided crow become a revelation of the oneness, the wonder, of all things. He suddenly knows that Nature is more than a flat, motionless scene beyond a glass window—no matter how beautiful from that point of view. The snow, the trees, the boiled egg, the wingbeat of the crow, the child, the woman, John himself are all included in the mystery which he experiences but cannot verbalize. His wife returns him to a world of less complex dimensions with the comment, "Eat your egg" (226), but the reader knows that this John will soon relive those awed moments when he was on the threshold of some kind of understanding.

There are other Johns and other searchers in the short stories, their experiences sometimes attesting not only the mystery of life but also the certainty of God's existence. But whatever the theme, there is always a delicate but certain buoyancy that lifts everyday experiences of Updike characters a bit above the ordinary. If man's immortality and God's reality are not clearly declared, they are hopefully implied. The search for their certainty never ceases.

There is the story of "The Astronomer," a bold, self-assured atheist who, though he usually overwhelms the scholarly Walter (another John) with his scientific certainties, reveals that he has had moments of fear. He tells of driving through the Southwestern United States and of feeling his insignificance against the vast, silent desert and its blank sky overhead. As he talks, his eyes reveal the fear he has felt. Walter's faith in God, though weak and flexible, coupled with the atheist's silent profession of uncertainty, blend to make the account a subtle proclamation of God's probability. The experience is recalled by the narrator "as if we were residents of a star suspended against the darkness of the city and the river" (186). Once again Updike uses a star to symbolize an unfathomable but permanent religious promise and, for contrast, employs the blackness of the city and the river at night to represent, symbolically, mankind's disbelief and ignorance.

"A Dying Cat," a highly symbolic and sophisticated "tale," repeats the explanation of immortality given by Caldwell in *The Centaur*. One living creature must die that another may live—that life may continue. In the short story, David Kern is the narrator. He tells about a restless walk on a night when his wife lies in labor at a nearby hospital in Oxford. He says of the experience, "It is a strange fact about Americans, that we tend to receive our supernatural mail on foreign soil—I helped a cat die. The incident had the signature: decisive but illegible" (253). David finds an injured cat in the street and lifts it carefully, laying it beside a hedge in a yard. Then, after placing an explanatory note under the cat's body, he goes home to read *The Everlasting Man*. The next day he learns that at the first hour of the morning when he had attended the dying cat, a perfect female infant had been born—to him. The story is an explanation through metaphor of Updike's concept of immortality. All things die that all may continue to live forever.

Another symbolic story which repeats a theme of one of the novels is "Churchgoing." Man's search for understanding, for a religion which can include his modern knowledge of life and death as well as his inherent desire to be singly significant in the universe, must be carried on through but beyond nineteenth-century Christian concepts. The church window, symbolizing the Church or Christianity beyond which Rabbit Angstrom seeks Truth in *Rabbit, Run*, reappears in "Churchgoing." David Kern tells of going to church on a Caribbean island. The service is dull and long, the hymns ponderous and a hundred years behind man's progress—something outmoded and useless except as unreasoned consolation. It is the windows of the ancient building which become figuratively meaningful.

For windows the church possessed tall arched apertures filled not with stained glass but with air and *outward vision*; [italics mine] . . . without moving from my pew I . . . could escape through those tall portals built to admit the breeze. I rested my eyes on earth's wide circle round. From this height the horizon of the sea was lifted halfway up the sky. The Caribbean seemed a steeply tilted blue plane to which the few fishing boats in the bay below had been attached like magnetized toys. God made the world, Aquinas says, in play. (252–53)

To find that God of Caribbean blue and splendor, that God who toyed the horizon into being and made the goats on the island—to discover the God who created man who questions, self-confined within the boundaries of man-made creeds and structures, one must look outward, through the windows of man's Christian edifice, and beyond it. Even the absence of stained glass seems meaningful. Do we need to remove some of the artificial stains, the "color," the blinders man has put into his religion so that we can see clearly with an "outward vision"? It seems certain that Updike's church windows suggest a need for new perception within the framework of modern religion, particularly Christianity.

That new vision is almost caught in "Pigeon Feathers," a title selection and the finest of the stories in the first three collections. The leading character is a fourteen-year-old boy who lives on a Pennsylvania farm. His name is David, but he seems to be the same boy who appears as Peter in *The Centaur* and who has been identified as John in the short stories reviewed here. He embodies the finest traits of all the young men in the category he represents. He is sensitive and serious, lonely and introspective. His family has moved to the farm from nearby Olinger, uprooting the boy from his home and his childhood in one gesture. Restless and agitated about the unfamiliar surroundings and the new life in which he finds himself, he searches for something to do. He will sort books—no, read. One book whose cover he has seen on the library shelf all his life is a comforting sight in the new surroundings: H. G. Wells, *The Outline of History*. In glancing through the second volume, David slips into the account of one political agitator, Jesus, "a kind of hobo, in a minor colony of the Roman Empire" (118). The account continues, upsetting the boy with every explanation.

By an accident impossible to reconstruct, he (the small *h* horrified David) survived his own crucifixion and presumably died a few weeks later. A religion was founded on the freakish incident. The credulous imagination of the times

restrospectively assigned miracles and supernatural preten-
sions to Jesus; a myth grew, and then a church. (118–19)

David is fascinated and terrified. He suddenly sees mankind, society, and his parents as frauds. He is thrown into
the adult world where all is a lie, a pretense, and a perplexity. Updike's theme of man's confusion resounds.
David is confused—man is confused—because of society's
failure, religion's failure, and each individual's failure.

The confusion is compounded for the boy when, a few
days later, he has a distinct vision of death in which he
sees his body slowly pressed and elongated and distorted
into the earth's strata. The fear of the cosmos in its
magnitude and its limitlessness, a theme which appears
in some of the Updike poetry, is repeated. One of the
consolations offered in the poetry is also renewed. In
"Mobile of Birds" man is consoled by the fact that even
though he is almost too tiny in relation to the universe to
be significant, he is essential just as the single bird is necessary to perfect balance of the mobile. An impression
similar to this finally makes its way through the confusion and fear; David feels "his first spark of comfort—too
small to be crushed" (124).

This conclusion is the beginning of the boy's climb
out of the dungeon of despair toward the bright assurance with which the story finally ends. Up to this point
he has not discussed his frantic terror. Now he goes eag-
erly to the catechetical class at the Lutheran Church.
Confident that the good man in the white collar will
comfort him, he bravely asks questions about the resurrection of the body, the dwelling place of the soul after
death, and the location of Heaven. The minister studi-
ously avoids answering David's questions, gazing at the
boy intently "with an awkward, puzzled flicker of forgiveness, as if there existed a secret between them that David
was violating" (133). There is created among the children a sense of "naughtiness occurring" (132) as the

minister, becoming a coward because he cannot answer the child's questions, transfers his shame to David. There is no better example anywhere in Updike's fiction of the failure of Christianity as man practices it and preaches it. It does not even answer the needs of a sincere, faithful child. As a matter of fact, it makes the child a sinner in the eyes of his peers simply because he yearns for truth. Its answers are inadequate for our time.

But David does not give up. He still feels that somewhere within his religion there is an answer. At home he studies his grandfather's Bible even though he detests the "apparatus of piety. Fusty churches, creaking hymns, ugly Sunday-school teachers and their stupid leaflets—he hated everything about them but the promise they held out, a promise that in the most perverse way . . . made every good and real thing, ball games and jokes and pert-breasted girls, possible" (135).

As the story progresses, David's fears change to anger. His mother cannot answer him. His father fails him by ignoring the serious nature of his questions. Like Harry Angstrom of *Rabbit, Run* and George Caldwell of *The Centaur*, he continues his search alone and unguided. When talking to his mother about the discussion with the minister regarding Heaven he says,

> "Well, I don't know. I want it to be *some*thing. I thought he'd tell me what it was. I thought that was his job." He was becoming angry, sensing her surprise at him. She had assumed that Heaven had faded from his head years ago. She had imagined that he had already entered, in the secrecy of silence, the conspiracy that he now knew to be all around him. (136)

David is a restless seeker after truth. His mother tries to dissuade him.

> "David," she asked gently, "don't you ever want to rest?"
> "No. Not forever."

"David, you're so young. When you get older, you'll feel differently."

"Grandpa didn't. Look how tattered this book is. (136)

And he does not rest. As his grandfather must have, he continues his search, renews his hope. Like Updike's other searchers, David continues to look to the Church, even after it has failed him. Updike's belief that within Christianity or beyond it lies a solution, appears once again. "The sight of clergymen cheered him; whatever they themselves thought, their collars were still a sign that somewhere, at some time, someone had recognized that we cannot, *cannot* submit to death" (140).

Finally a second comfort presents itself. Another Updike theme unfolds. The little everyday wonders may lead to some answers. It is the little things that bring joy. One of these is David's dog—not just the animal's patience and love for the boy but something more startling —more *sure*.

The dog's ears, laid flat against his skull in fear, were folded so intricately, so—he groped for the concept—*surely*. Where the dull-studded collar made the fur stand up, each hair showed a root of soft white under the length, black-tipped, of the metal-color that had lent the dog its name. In his agitation Copper panted through nostrils that were elegant slits, like two healed cuts, or like the keyholes of a dainty lock of black, grained wood. His whole whorling, knotted, jointed body was a wealth of such embellishments. (142)

Even the dog's fur has been planned. There is no doubt. *Something* planned it. Something there is which needs understanding.

The last section of this intricately conceived, perfectly developed story begins with an intricately conceived, perfectly developed line: "A barn in a day, is a small night" (144). The figure of speech in the disciplined line of poetry is a preview of the scenes to follow. The reader senses an approaching revelation, a climax for the story, the summit of experiences for David and all the young men he represents.

Still silently searching for comfort and answers, still trying to expand his religious beliefs to fit his needs, the boy goes about his tasks on the farm. His grandmother, fearing damage to useless furniture stored in the barn, wants him to shoot the pigeons nesting in its rafters. David insists that he doesn't "want to kill anything especially" (143), but the action of firing the gun and successfully carrying out the distasteful mission helps him vent his anger at the world, prepares him for a silent discovery which is both the end of his struggle and, the reader feels, the beginning of a faith which will satisfy his needs.

When the birds are dead, David comes out of the barn, the "small night" of carnage, and his dawn begins. He digs a hole near the wild strawberry plants and, kneeling, drops in the pigeons one at a time. Silently examining each pliant body, he discovers the intricate and elaborate design of its feathers. The colors and textures are even more remarkable than his dog's hair had seemed, "each filament . . . shaped within the shape of the feather, and the feathers in turn . . . trimmed to fit a pattern that flowed without error across the bird's body" (149). No two are alike. He ponders the fact that such beauty is spent on millions of useless birds, beauty "executed, it seemed, in a controlled rapture, with a joy that hung level in the air above and behind him" (149). When the last body is covered, he rises.

Crusty coverings were lifted from him, and with a feminine, slipping sensation along his nerves that seemed to give the air hands, he was robed in this certainty: that the God who had lavished such craft upon these worthless birds would not destroy His whole Creation by refusing to let David live forever. (149–50)

The young boy *experiences* knowledge. God exists. There are answers. Life—his life—will go on forever. Triumphantly, exultantly, the story of David is concluded. His questions have not all been answered; his search has only begun. To question—to search—to wish to know, and now and then to be "robed in certainty" by the discovery of so wonderful an answer as pigeon feathers—is to begin to know.

In *The Music School,* the fourth volume of short stories, very few of the characters "begin to know." Most of them are suffering from life's complexity, and most are searching, one way or another, for a way out of their bewilderment. In these stories (and in the fourth and fifth novels which are chronological neighbors), a new dimension of the search theme develops. The characters are, in general, older than those of *Pigeon Feathers, The Same Door,* and *Olinger Stories.* Their quandaries are those of the young-to-middle-aged who are experienced in marriage and sex. They search for some kind of sex utopia. Eight of the twenty stories in *The Music School* deal with the dilemmas of illicit love affairs, dissatisfaction with a mate, emotional disturbances growing out of divided loyalties between the wife to whom one is pledged and the mistress whom his sexual appetite demands. Sexual conflicts create the perplexities which give the search theme a new impetus.

Sex, a topic more fully explored in *Couples,* appears in *The Music School* as the principal cause of man's perpetual state of bewilderment. Many of his problems stem from his unwillingness or inability to relate over a long period of time to one and the same sex partner. Love has many facets, most of them reflecting sex drives, each of these a slightly different cut. The jewel of life is many-sided. As it turns in the sun, man sees the beauty of first one reflection and then another, each a seemingly perfect cut of the gem until another catches his eye. Society says, "select one"; he is unable to limit himself, and complete confusion is the result. Searching for a solution to his dilemma, he usually finds, instead, still another glittering sex experience which in turn will fade when the light strikes a newer one—or such is the overall impression of the stories in *The Music School*.

"My Lover Has Dirty Finger Nails" (*The Music School*, 164) is a typical example. In this case it is a woman who has grown tired of her husband sexually, who has a lover she is trying to forget, and who has met a psychiatrist who promises to be her next jewel. Her problem is boredom in sex. Her continued search is for a new man, not for a solution to her problems.

In the title selection, "The Music School," Alfred Schweigen tells his own story. He begins by saying, "I exist in time" (183). Immediately we know that he is a man of our time—or of any time in which one must exist as that era dictates. He relates several of the circumstances which make up the texture of his life: a tragically meaningless murder about which he has heard but can do nothing, a trusting daughter to whom he is committed, forced compliance with a bold change in a sacred church ritual which, supposedly ordained by God, had existed unquestioned for more than a thousand years, a wife who visits a psychiatrist because of his unfaithfulness—all circumstances which hold him and shape his life, he thinks, without his influence. He just "exists in time." He comments, "Each moment I live, I must think where to place my fingers, and press them down with no confidence of hearing a chord" (189–90). He is unaware that he gives his life any direction; he is adrift in a stream of humanity. He continues: "My friends are like me. We are all pilgrims, faltering toward divorce" (190). Life is a perplexity over which we have no control. Together we are swept toward divorce with the tide of the time. There is little promise that arriving there, we will be any better off, however. Choices are made for us, and we are forced to accept them. All is one chaotic sequence of loves and hates in which we are forced to take part but on which we have no influence and for which we can accept no responsibility.

In these sex-problem stories there are a few "victims" of life who make an effort to correct their errors and to understand themselves. Updike's searchers of integrity reappear. "Leaves" tells of near madness experienced by a young man who, in his search, tries to return to the wife he had wronged and left. His vision begins to clear when he looks outward toward nature for assistance. Another of Updike's themes unfolds: nature has some answers. The young man says, "It comes upon me as strange, after the long darkness of self-absorption and fear and shame in which I have been living, that things are beautiful, that independent of our catastrophes they continue to maintain the casual precision, the effortless abundance of inventive 'effect,' which is the hallmark and specialty of Nature. Nature: this morning it seems to me very clear that Nature may be defined as that which exists without guilt" (52). Updike themes of human perplexity, the beauty of little things, perpetual search, and Nature as a possible answer all emerge. The theme of search leads in significance and continues.

The finest story in this collection, one which does not dwell on sexual maladjustment, is "The Hermit." In the same way that the short stories seem to be the climax of Updike's fiction, this one among them becomes the pinnacle of the entire pyramid. It includes the dominant Updike themes, relegates each to its deserved position in relation to the others, and reaches an "exhaltation" of good things in life before all is plunged into an abyss of despair. Not quite closing the door on hope, it nevertheless suggests that the man who tries to discover life in its most exquisite purity and who reaches a threshold of understanding or fulfillment is so rare that society will destroy him. "The Hermit" tells about a searcher who almost finds something. It is the soul and summit of Updike's art.

Updike themes found in this one treasure of a short story are all carefully laced and interlaced into a delicate but elaborate pattern, a rich fabric textured and shaded, finished without flaw. We detect first the familiar thread of thought—*each man is alone*—when we meet one of Updike's most isolated individuals, Stanley, an outcast intellectually dull, physically repulsive, socially inept. Stanley is aware of his inadequacies, of the "something he could not quite believe was as simple as stupidity [which] clouded his apprehension" (239). Whatever it is, the "something" makes living with "normal" people a constant trial for others and for himself. The second theme develops: *Man is forever perplexed.* Life is one competition after another, and Stanley always loses. It is as if his mind were "too finely adjusted to bear the jostle of others, to function in the heavy damp climate human activity bred" (240). The only solution is to walk away from the confusion. He does, burrowing deep into the woods to build a hovel and a way of life he can tolerate.

His problems are not immediately solved, but step by step as he looks to nature to fulfill his needs, he finds answers to questions hardly asked. He does not always understand the message but is comforted by the texture of the hieroglyphics. His mind becomes "a beautiful foreign book whose illustrations [are] enhanced, in precision and wonder, by the unintelligibility of the text" (254). *Nature can help solve our dilemmas.* A third theme is threaded into the web.

The subtheme of sex as one cause of man's quandary appears here but is relegated to a reasonable place in this story. Stanley has known women, needs them even after his departure from "civilized" living, but as with no other Updike character, this outcast relieves his body and his life of the sexual appetite by eliminating the need to be admired. Sexual activity had been a preening, a self-gratuity, an acceptance of approval. Learning to live apart from others, he needs no approval. Even self-admiration is not necessary. Stanley breaks his mirror and buries it. When no one looks at him, when he is not judged even by his own reflection in a mirror, no preening is necessary. Sex can be forgotten and is. The sex theme is shaded into a subordinate position.

Stanley's isolation gives him new stature. We are reminded of the theme of man's significance as a part of the intricate and complex total of all things. In his island of silence in the woods, Stanley becomes a man singly blessed, a creature select, a nonentity exalted to the very pinnacle of the thrust toward God. In no other Updike story is the point so distinctly made that *in our slenderest tenuity are we significant*. Except during infrequent visits of those from the outer world of town, Stanley is the only human in his environment. There is no one else to compete with him for God's attention. One to one is the richest possible ratio, the most direct relationship. Stanley is elevated to such a position in his solitary seclusion.

Not only does he have dignity and significance, but the tiniest creature or plant or breath of air is important as well. Updike's motif of the value of little things sings out in the lyric prose. In Stanley's retreat, a vein in a leaf spells beauty. Contrasts between the weathered weed and the new pine boards in his shack are worth studying. Minute sounds create delicate music. Joy erupts in him at the sight of a patch of sky or a ripple of pure water. He becomes "aware, intensely, of tiny distinctions—shades of brown and gray in the twigs, differences in the shapes of leaves, the styles of growing" (253–54). Nothing is unimportant. *All things have purpose.*

The search theme is the spine of "The Hermit." Stanley's search is the most deliberate and yet the most natural in all the Updike short stories. The unhappy man cannot continue to cope with life as he has known it and sets out to find a way of living which has meaning for him. His search is as natural as that of an animal seeking shelter from a storm. There is something Stanley needs, and he seeks it. If he were asked to define it, he perhaps would say, "peace" or "quiet," certainly not anything so philosophic as "identity" or "relationship to the cosmos." His *search is intuitive*, not intellectual. He moves away from confusion, takes care of his simple bodily needs, and waits. After months of shedding the encumbrances of habit and the clutter of thought, he learns to be a part of the silence surrounding him.

In this silence, he hears. Each morning he wakes "with a sense of having been called" (257). There is no effort on his part to explore mysticism or to reach anything or even to listen. He simply hears. Eventually the voice of silence becomes an impression of "infinite gentleness and urgency" (257). The experience is apart from his efforts, not a self-searching, not an outreaching, not something he has imagined, for he is a stolid, slow-thinking man. It is other-oriented, entirely apart from his willing. *Something* communicates with *him*.

Updike's most auspicious theme emerges: *God exists.* This is not a god of man's making. This is not a theologized and verbalized God. Stanley does not create Him. The author daringly declares his belief. God is there— not in man, not of man, not designed or defined or encompassed by man's vocabulary or man's intellect, but God Present, God Alone, God One.

In this story as in no other, Karl Barth's influence is apparent. This twentieth-century theologian whose name appears occasionally in Updike works and in whose thought-waves Updike frequently seems to exist, does not believe man can find God by any self-searching, any other-seeking, or any intellectual, emotional, or mystical pursuit. God can reach man, but man cannot of his own will reach God. If he could, he would diminish God to the limited scope of man's concept of Him. Man's "search" can be only a readiness. God must do the reaching. In "The Hermit" a "vaporous presence" (258) makes itself felt by a simple, waiting man who had not known what it was he sought. No verbalized definition of God clutters his mind. No moralized "search" drives him. Only intuition readies him.

After several episodes of awareness of a Presence, Stanley, like Harry Angstrom of *Rabbit, Run*, who knew there was "something that wanted him to find it," realizes that there is "something that want[s] to be answered" (258). He feels it as "an overwhelming fineness in things; the minute truth of bark textures, the many-layered translucence of leaves, the stately gliding intervals between tree trunks" (258). He does not know its vocabulary. He cannot speak to it. The only response he can make by way of an answer is to wait. He waits. He waits again and again. Finally he is rewarded. "A silence embraced all phenomena; the sound beneath the silence approached." Stanley leans against a tree and waits with a "joy indistinguishable from fear" (259). He is ready to know.

But in the story's tragic conclusion, the artist permits no final revelation. At the moment of discovery, a man on the threshold of understanding is jerked back into the meanness of life as lived by "reasonable" people. An empty, crystal vessel waiting to be filled, he is shattered suddenly, irrevocably. His waiting is over; the moment of knowing is gone. The sound beneath the silence will not be heard amidst the clamor and clatter of civilized confinement to which he will be returned.

The critics who say that Updike has "nothing to say" [6] have not read "The Hermit."

Sharing the agony of Stanley's loss, the reader is nevertheless still free to question. What is the author's message? Is Stanley's fate the lot of man? To exist in conflict, to seek to know God, perhaps even to reach a threshold of understanding only to be thrust back into chaos—is this man's fate? The optimistic tone of Updike's earlier works is not present here. Hope has no place in Stanley's world. Has it a place in any man's world?

The Updike message in this story is not that there is hope for the Stanleys who wait quietly because they don't know what else to do with their lives. It is not even hopeful for the conscious searchers who tirelessly turn the pages of wisdom and perpetually peer into the clouded sky of mysticism. They are destined to fruitless seeking, for man cannot of his own will reach God. And yet the message is hopeful. It is simply that God exists. To believe we can reach Him is our folly. To be reached by Him is our chance in ten million. To search for Him without reward is our destiny. That He exists is our hope.

John Updike is one of the most important writers on the contemporary scene because of his superb literary artistry and because he has something to say. He is followed closely by the reading public because he is a searcher of integrity, one who accepts no for an answer when no is the answer. Accordingly, the yes aspects of his assertions are valid, too. Yes, there is some virtue in man. Yes, goodness lives. Yes, the individual is significant, at least minutely. He may even be intuitively aware that God seeks him. Yes, life in all its complexity can be good.

The thing man needs in order to accept both the negative and the positive truths is a concept of God which allows for all life's discrepancies, ambiguities, and changes. The search for such a concept, the search for a religion for our time, is the philosophic goal of the artist, Updike. There is much, much yet to learn and much yet to write, but for the moment, the assertion that God exists is the most important of John Updike's "yea sayings."

Notes

1 — Perspective

1. Frank Kappler, "Existentialism," *Life*, November 6, 1964, pp. 92–94.
2. John Updike, from a personal conversation, June 10, 1965.

3 — The Poorhouse Fair

1. Stanley J. Rowland, Jr., "The Limits of Littleness," rev. of *Pigeon Feathers*, by John Updike, *Christian Century*, 79, July 4, 1962, p. 840.
2. Michael Novak, "Updike's Quest for Liturgy," *Commonweal*, 78, May 10, 1963, p. 192.
3. John Updike. Quoted by Judith Serebnick, "New Creative Writers," *Library Journal*, 134, February 1, 1959, p. 499.
4. David Galloway, "The Absurd Man as Saint: The Novels of John Updike," *Modern Fiction Studies*, 10 (Summer 1964), p. 112.

5 — The Centaur

1. Richard Gilman, "The Youth of An Author," *New Republic*, 148, April 13, 1963, p. 27.
2. David Galloway, "The Absurd Man As Saint: The Novels of John Updike," *Modern Fiction Studies*, 10 (Summer 1964), p. 121.
3. Ibid., p. 125.
4. Paul A. Doyle, "Updike's Fiction: Motifs and Techniques," *Catholic World*, 199 (September 1964), p. 356.

5. Richard Gilman, "The Youth of An Author," *New Republic*, 148, April 12, 1963, p. 25.

6 – Of the Farm

1. David Galloway, "The Absurd Man as Saint: The Novels of John Updike," *Modern Fiction Studies*, 10 (Summer 1964), p. 122.

7 – Couples

1. Paul Tillich, "Frontiers," *Journal of Bible and Religion* 33, No. 1. (January 1965) p. 17.
2. John Updike, "The Dogwood Tree: A Boyhood," *Assorted Prose* (New York, 1965), pp. 180–84.
3. Richard E. Beard, "Dr. and Mrs. Solidarity" (oil painting), Northern Illinois University Faculty Show, Northern Illinois University, DeKalb, Illinois, 1967.
4. Paul Tillich, "The Good That I Will, I Do Not," *The Eternal Now* (New York, 1963), p. 56.
5. Paul Tillich, "Man and Earth," *The Eternal Now* (New York, 1963), p. 72.
6. Paul Tillich, "Forgetting and Being Forgotten," *The Eternal Now* (New York, 1963), p. 33.

8 – The Short Stories

1. Guerin La Course, "The Innocence of John Updike," *Commonweal*, 77, February 8, 1963, p. 512.
2. John Updike, "Foreword," *Olinger Stories* (New York, 1954), p. v.
3. Irving Howe, "Mass Society and Post-Modern Fiction," *Recent American Fiction*, ed. Joseph Waldmeir (Boston, 1963), p. 14.
4. Stanley J. Rowland, Jr., "The Limits of Littleness" rev. of *Pigeon Feathers*, by John Updike, *Christian Century*, 79, July 4, 1962, pp. 840–41.
5. Ibid., p. 841.
6. John W. Aldridge, "Cultivating Corn Out of Season," *Book Week*, November 21, 1965, p. 5.

Selected Bibliography

Aldridge, John W. "Cultivating Corn Out of Season," *Book Week,* November 21, 1965, p. 5.

Beard, Richard E. "Dr. and Mrs. Solidarity" (oil painting), Northern Illinois University Faculty Show, Northern Illinois University, De Kalb, Illinois, 1967.

Doyle, Paul A. "Updike's Fiction: Motifs and Techniques," *Catholic World,* 199 (September 1964), pp. 356–62.

Galloway, David D. "The Absurd Man as Saint: The Novels of John Updike," *Modern Fiction Studies,* 10, No. 2 (Summer 1964), pp. 111–27.

Gilman, Richard. "The Youth Of An Author," *New Republic,* April 13,1963, pp. 25–27.

Howard, J. "Can a Nice Novelist Finish First?" *Life,* 61, November 4, 1966, pp. 74–74A.

Howe, Irving, "Mass Society and Post-Modern Fiction," *Recent American Fiction,* ed. Joseph J. Waldmeir. Boston, 1963.

Kappler, Frank. "Existentialism," *Life,* November 6, 1964, pp. 86–110.

La Course, Guerin. "The Innocence of John Updike," *Commonweal,* 77, February 8, 1963, pp. 512–14.

Novak, Michael. "Updike's Quest For Liturgy," *Commonweal,* 78, May 10, 1963, 192–95.

Rowland, Stanley J., Jr. "The Limits of Littleness" rev. of *Pigeon Feathers,* by John Updike, *Christian Century,* 79, July 4, 1962, pp. 840–41.

Serebnick, Judith. "New Creative Writers," *Library Journal,* 84, February 1, 1959, p. 499.

Tillich, Paul. *The Eternal Now.* New York, 1956.

————. "Frontiers," *Journal of Bible and Religion* 33, No. 1 (January 1965) p. 17.

Updike, John. *Assorted Prose*. New York, 1965.

————. *The Carpentered Hen and Other Tame Creatures*. New York, 1958.

————. *The Centaur*. New York, 1963.

————. *Couples*. New York, 1968.

————. *The Music School*. New York, 1966.

————. *Of the Farm*. New York, 1965.

————. *Olinger Stories*. New York, 1954.

————. *Pigeon Feathers*. New York, 1962.

————. *The Poorhouse Fair*. New York, 1959.

————. *Rabbit, Run*. New York, 1960.

————. *The Same Door*. New York, 1959.

————. *Verse, The Carpentered Hen and Other Tame Creatures and Telephone Poles and Other Poems*. Greenwich, Conn., 1965.

Updike, John and Nancy Ekholm Burkert. *A Child's Calendar*. New York, 1965.

Updike, John and Warren Chappell. *The Magic Flute*. New York, 1962.

————. *The Ring*. New York, 1964.

Index

DATE DUE